GOD
is Good

...and Good Means Good

GOD
is Good

...and Good Means Good

Diane Kannady

TruCONNECTIONS
PRESS

DEDICATION

This book is dedicated to the Riches in Christ family. Without your love, friendship, prayers, and support, this book would not have been possible. Thank you.

May we continue to run our race so that we finish our course in a way that brings maximum glory to God and maximum good to as many people as possible.

CONTENTS

FOREWORD

"Be diligent to present yourself approved to God as a workman who does not need to be ashamed, handling accurately the word of truth" (2 Timothy 2:15, NASB).

I cannot think of a better way to describe Diane Kannady to you than with the above scripture. I agreed to write the foreword for this book because Diane is one of the most dedicated and anointed teachers of the Word of God that I have known in over 30 years of ministry. Her diligence to studying and rightly dividing God's Word has consistently been evident. When I learned that Diane was writing this book, I knew it would be a great benefit to the body of Christ. *God is Good...and Good Means Good* will open your eyes to spiritual truths that will impact your life and ministry.

I first met Diane 20 years ago when she came to visit a Sunday service at our church, Trinity. My wife and I always have an eye out for people who have a special call on their lives. From our very first conversation with Diane, we could see that she was one of those people.

Over the last 20 years, Diane has preached many times at our church and at many of the churches in the St. Louis area. She has been a conference speaker for us and many others. We have always been amazed at how she takes God's Word, breaks it down, and effectively presents it as a teacher and a gifted communicator. She has been teaching at her ministry, Riches in Christ, every Friday evening at Trinity since March 6, 1992.

The place Diane's giftedness perhaps shines the brightest is as one of our primary lecturers at City Bible Institute (CBI). It is important to me that our students get the best. Our students love her teaching style and substance. This book is an elaboration of material she taught in the CBI course, "The Character of God."

So, get ready to be blessed. *God is Good...and Good Means Good* is worth reading, studying, and sharing with others.

Rev. Dr. Joel A. Oliver
Senior Pastor of Trinity Assembly of God Church
President of City Bible Institute

INTRODUCTION

Troubles, trials, tests, tribulation, and suffering do not come from God. How can I make such a bold statement? Because that is what Jesus said when He was on this earth: *"The thief* (the devil) *comes only to steal and kill and destroy; I* (Jesus) *have come that they* (my people) *may have life, and have it to the full"* (John 10:10, NIV). According to Jesus, good comes from God and bad comes from the devil.

If there's something in your life that is bad, it did not come from God. I realize that statement brings up many "Yes, but what about…?" questions. Yes, but what about Job? Yes, but what about God's sovereignty? Yes, but what about the Old Testament? All of these can be answered from the Bible. We will deal with these and other questions in the following pages.

WHY DO WE NEED TO DISCUSS THIS SUBJECT?

- People become angry and bitter at God for allowing the hardships they face and they struggle with how a loving God could permit such a thing.

- When we're not sure if our troubles come from God or the devil, we respond to life's challenges with uncertainty: "God, if this trial is from you, I submit to it and to whatever you are trying to teach me. Devil, if this is from you, I resist you in Jesus' name." This is a position of weakness, not strength.

- When people believe that God is somehow responsible for their difficulties, many end up angry at God.

- As Christians, we are called to live and walk by faith. Part of living by faith is trusting God. You cannot fully trust someone you believe has harmed you or will harm you in any way. That's where many of us are—struggling to trust a Being we're not certain we can fully rely on. Psalm 9:10 says, "And they that know thy name will put their trust in thee." The word "name" has the idea of character. Those who know God's character, those who know what He is truly like, will put their trust in Him.

Accurate knowledge of God's character will produce in your heart an unshakeable confidence in God. Through this book, by God's grace, you will learn that the Bible clearly teaches that God is good…and good means good.

GOD IS GOOD...
AND GOOD MEANS GOOD

*M*ost Christians would say they believe God is good. When the preacher says "God is a good God," we all nod our heads in agreement and shout "Amen!" But in the next breath, we hear people turn around and say that God let their friend have a car wreck to teach him a lesson or He gave their loved one a disease to keep that person humble. Ask yourself, "Is a car wreck good?" "Is a disease good?"

When the word "good" is used in everyday conversation, it means an experience that is beneficial, helpful, or pleasant. But when "good" is used in connection with God, our thinking often changes. Something bad happens and we say it's good because we believe God allowed it, permitted it, or is behind it in some way. Even though we may not think our situation is good, we reason that because the circumstance came through the hand of God, it must be good because He knows best.

But here's the question we need to answer: What does the Bible mean when it says God is good? Several years ago I decided to find out. "Good" appears in 655 verses in the Bible. I read each verse and made an amazing discovery. Every time the word "good" is used in scripture, it means *good*. It means what you and I understand the word to mean when we use it in our daily conversations.

WHY ARE WE CONFUSED?

Much of what we believe about God and the word "good" comes from looking at our experiences or the experiences of others and trying to explain why they happened. For example, Aunt Mary has a car wreck and people assume that God allowed the accident so Mary could share the gospel with the ambulance workers on the way to the hospital. Therefore, the car wreck is good. But if an earthly father cut the brake line on his child's car to give him a chance to preach to the paramedics, we'd call that bad—and we'd be right. Yet, people regularly credit a good God with negative and destructive circumstances.

Others might call Aunt Mary's car wreck a "blessing in disguise" because good came out of it—one of the paramedics received Christ. But God doesn't cause bad in order to bring good out of it. When Jesus healed a blind and dumb man by casting a devil out of him, the Pharisees accused Jesus of casting out devils by the power of the devil. Jesus' response was that if Satan casts out Satan then his kingdom is divided against itself (Matthew 12:24-26). According to Jesus, the devil doesn't work against himself. Well, neither does God. God does not cause our troubles only to turn around and deliver us from them.

In fact, the Bible says that God comforts us in our troubles. *"Who comforts us in all our troubles, so that we can comfort those in any trouble with the comfort we ourselves received from God"* (2 Corinthians 1:4, NIV). The Bible also says God delivers us out of all of our afflictions. *"Many are the afflictions of the righteous: but the Lord delivereth him out of them all"* (Psalm 34:19). If God sends trouble into our lives only to comfort us in the midst of them or if He afflicts us only to deliver us, then His house is divided and He is working against Himself.

Although God doesn't send bad circumstances into our lives, the Bible does teach that He can take genuine evil and bring genuine good out of it. Romans 8:28 says, *"And we know that God causes all things to work together for good to those who love God, to those who are called according to His purpose"* (NASB). This is what happened to Aunt Mary. God didn't cause her car wreck, but He did bring genuine good out of genuine bad in Aunt Mary's difficulty.

You Have To Read In Context

Many wrong ideas about God and the word "good" come from Bible verses and phrases taken out of context. Suppose you wrote a letter to me and I simply read one line or phrase instead of reading the entire letter. I could easily misunderstand what you're saying because I've taken your words out of the setting in which you intended them. I've taken them out of context. In the same way, we can't pull one line or phrase from the Bible and try to apply it to our individual circumstances. We must learn to read the Bible in context.

When something bad happens to us, we often try to find out the reason why. We may remember hearing that God chastens people. *"For whom the Lord loveth he chasteneth, and scourgeth every son whom he receiveth"* (Hebrews 12:6). So we decide that our difficult circumstance must be God's way of chastening us. However, if we read Hebrews 12:6 in context, we find that the Lord chastens us with His Word, not with troubles and trials. We'll discuss this verse more fully in a later chapter.

Maybe you've heard the statement, "It rains on the just and the unjust." When people use this phrase, they usually mean God brings rain (or bad things) into the lives of everyone, good and bad people alike. But these words are found in a verse that has nothing to do with God bringing or allowing bad things in people's lives: *"But I say unto you, Love your enemies, bless them that curse you, do good to them that hate you, and pray for them which despitefully use you, and persecute you; That ye may be the children of your Father which is in heaven: for he maketh his sun to rise on the evil and on the good, and sendeth rain on the just and on the unjust"* (Matthew 5:44-45). The point of the verse is to be kind to those who wrong us because that is how our Father in heaven acts. He is kind to the evil and the good. God gives both of them sunshine and rain to grow the crops they need to survive. This verse has nothing to do with God bringing bad into people's lives. In fact, it means exactly the opposite.

When trouble strikes, it's common to hear people say, "God won't give you more than you can bear." But this idea is also based on part of a verse taken out of context: *"And God is faithful; he will not let you be tempted beyond what you can bear. But when you are tempted, he will also provide a way out so that you can stand up under it"* (1 Corinthians 10:13, NIV). The focus of this verse is sin, not trials from God. Let's take a closer look.

In 1 Corinthians 10:7-11, Paul the Apostle lists four major sins committed by the Israelites when they left Egypt: idolatry, fornication, tempting Christ, and murmuring. Paul warns the Corinthians to take heed that they do not fall into the same sins (verse 12). He goes on to say in verse 13 that we all get tempted with these same things. Paul makes the point that God never allows us to be tempted above what we can bear because He always makes a way for us to escape the sin if we'll take it. The passage has nothing to do with trials and tribulation being brought into our lives by God. It has nothing to do with God "not giving us more trouble than we can bear."

› ➔➤➤▸ · ◂◄◄◄ ‹

God is a good God. The question is: What does the word "good" mean? Every time "good" is used in the Bible, it means what you and I understand the word to mean. We must let the Bible define "good" in connection with God—not our experience, someone else's experience, or parts of verses taken out of context.

JESUS SHOWS US THAT GOD IS GOOD...
AND GOOD MEANS GOOD

To see God clearly and to get an accurate picture of His character, we must understand how to read the Bible. Everything the Bible tells us about God must be read and understood in the light of Jesus. We don't start our study of how God treats people with Job or with Noah's flood or with the lady who died even though the entire church prayed for her to be healed. We start our study with Jesus. Hebrews 1:1-2 says that *"In the past God spoke to our forefathers through the prophets at many times and in various ways, but in these last days he has spoken to us by his Son"* (NIV). Jesus, the Word made flesh, is God's message to us.

When one of the disciples asked Jesus to show them the Father, Jesus replied, *"Anyone who has seen me has seen the Father"* (John 14:9, NIV). Jesus showed them the Father, not because Jesus *is* the Father, but because He spoke the words of His Father and did the works of His Father by the power of the Father in Him. In fact, Jesus said He only did what He saw His Father do. *"I tell you the truth, the Son can do nothing by himself; he can do only what he sees his Father doing, because whatever the Father does the Son also does"* (John 5:19, NIV). If you want to know what God is like, what God does, and how

He treats people, you must look at Jesus and what He shows us about God. (See Note 1 at the end of the book for more scripture references on the works of Jesus.)

Many people believe God sends or allows troubles and afflictions to teach us, purge us, perfect us, test us, and chasten us. But if our only source of information about God is what Jesus shows us about the Father, we could never conclude that God is behind the hardships of life. Think about what Jesus did when He was on this earth. He healed people. He set people free from bondage. He taught people the Word of God. He cast out devils. He raised people from the dead. He fed people. He met the needs of people. He encouraged and comforted people. He had compassion on people.

Notice what Jesus *did not* do. He didn't make anyone sick or refuse to heal one person who came to Him. He didn't set up circumstances to test people. He didn't send trials to teach people. He didn't send storms, He stopped them. He didn't cause donkey cart crashes and He didn't send a single blessing in disguise. Jesus did none of the things people regularly credit God with doing.

We asked this question in the last chapter: What does the word "good" mean when it is used in connection with God in the Bible? Good is defined as the kind of actions Jesus performed when He was on earth. Acts 10:38 says, *"How God anointed Jesus of Nazareth with the Holy Ghost and with power: who went about **doing good**, and healing all that were oppressed of the devil; for God was with Him."*

Through His teachings, Jesus authorized us to understand God in terms of a good earthly Father. *"Or what man is there of you, whom if his son ask bread, will he give him a stone? Or if he ask a fish, will he give him a serpent? If ye then, being evil, know how to give good gifts unto your children, how much more shall your Father which is in heaven give good things to them that ask him?"* (Matthew 7:9-11). Jesus says our heavenly Father is better than the best earthly father. What good earthly father would give his child a sickness to discipline him? What good earthly father would let his son's house burn down to teach him a lesson? Based on what Jesus shows and tells us about God, we can say with certainty that if you would not create tragedy in your own child's life or in the life of someone you love, then God will not bring troubles to you.

⋅ →꘎꘎꘎ ⋅ ꘎꘎꘎← ⋅

Jesus said He only does what He sees His Father do. This means if Jesus does something, the Father does it too. And it means if Jesus does not do it, God does not do it either. Jesus shows us and tells us that the trials and hardships of life do not come from God because God is good...and good means good.

WHERE DO TRIALS
AND TROUBLES COME FROM?

*B*efore we deal with several of the "Yes, but what about…?" questions that often come up during discussions about life's trials and challenges, we first need to examine why afflictions and troubles are here in the earth.

LIFE IN A SIN CURSED EARTH

When God completed His work of creation, He surveyed it and declared it to be very good. *"And God saw everything that he had made, and, behold, it was very good"* (Genesis 1:31). Remember what the word "good" means. It means *good*. In God's original creation, there was no sickness and death, no killer storms, no corruption, no poison in ivy, no earthquakes, or any other form of destruction. Everything was very good.

When Adam and Eve disobeyed God in the Garden of Eden, their sin had a significant impact on God's creation—on both the human race and the earth itself. Death entered the world through Adam's sin: *"When Adam sinned, sin entered the entire human race. His sin spread death throughout all the world, so everything began to grow old and die"* (Romans 5:12, TLB). Because of Adam's sin, a curse came into the earth. *"Cursed is the ground because of you; In toil you shall eat of it all the days of your life"* (Genesis 3:17, NASB). *It will grow thorns and thistles for you, and you shall eat its grasses. All your life you will sweat to master it, until your dying day. Then you will return to the ground from which you came"* (Genesis 3:18-19, TLB).

The natural laws at work in the earth today are largely the result of Adam's sin and its effect on creation. Jesus said it this way, *"Lay not up for yourselves treasures upon earth, where moth and rust doth corrupt, and where thieves break through and steal"* (Matthew 6:19). We now live in an earth where moths chew holes in cloth and rust eats through metal. If you set a tomato on the kitchen table and leave it there, it will rot. Not because God made tomatoes to rot, but because death and corruption entered the world through Adam's sin and they are at work in the earth.

Every day we must deal with the consequences of sin and its effects in the earth and the human race. That means killer storms, weeds, rust, decay, and death are now part of the earth's makeup. We also have bodies that are mortal and subject to sickness, old age, and death. We must interact with people who make unwise and sinful choices that can directly affect our lives. And we have an enemy, the devil, who seeks to destroy us. All of these elements combine to produce the hardships and difficulties we face in this life. Yes, suffering is present in this world, but it does not come from God. It is the result of living in an earth that has been radically altered by sin.

THE DEVIL AND GOD...BUDDIES?

Some say, "That's right, God doesn't do bad to people, but He allows the devil to do it. After all, the devil is God's devil

12

and the Lord sometimes allows him to afflict us in order to test us, teach us, and perfect us." God and the devil are not on the same side. They aren't working together. The Bible never calls the devil an ally of God, an instrument of God, or God's teaching tool. The devil is called an "enemy" or an "adversary." The name Satan means "adversary." *Strong's Concordance* calls him "the archenemy of good."

James 4:7 says, *"Submit yourselves therefore to God. Resist the devil, and he will flee from you."* If God sends the devil to teach and discipline you, then how can you obey this verse and *resist* the devil yet still receive the teaching, discipline, and purging from God *through* the devil? You can't. "Yes," some would say, "but what about Job? God turned the devil loose on Job, didn't He?" No, God did not turn the devil loose on Job. We'll discuss Job's story in a later chapter.

Trials, tribulations, persecutions, afflictions, hardships, and suffering do not come from God. Jesus told the parable of the sower sowing the Word and said that Satan brings trials, afflictions, and persecutions to steal the Word of God from men: *"The sower soweth the word. And these are they by the way side, where the word is sown; but when they have heard, Satan cometh immediately, and taketh away the word that was sown in their hearts. And these are they likewise which are sown on stony ground; who, when they have heard the word, immediately receive it with gladness; And have no root in themselves, and so endure but for a time: afterward, when **affliction** or **persecution** ariseth for the word's sake, immediately they are offended"* (Mark 4:14-17). Matthew's account of this parable says: *"Yet hath he not root in himself, but dureth for a while: for when **tribulation** or **persecution** ariseth because of the word, by and by he is offended"* (Matthew 13:21).

Satan attempts to steal the Word of God from us through the hardships of life. Here's how this happens. All of us have been in situations that make it look like God has forgotten about us or doesn't love us. We've all had circumstances that try to convince us that we aren't going to make it. But according to what God says, He hasn't forgotten about us. He loves us and He promises to get us through until He gets us out. In hard times, we face the temptation to agree with what we see and feel rather than with what God says in the Bible. Satan is called the tempter (1 Thessalonians 3:5) and in the midst of our troubles—through thoughts of doubt and discouragement—he puts pressure on us to abandon God's Word. If we accept the thoughts that tell us God doesn't love us, that He's forgotten us, and that we're not going to make it, then we've let go of God's Word. Satan has successfully stolen the Word from us. (See Note 2 for more details about Satan's origin and work.)

, →》》》 · 《《《← ‹

As you face the difficulties of life, it's important to know that your troubles do not come from God. Hardships, tribulation, troubles, and trials are part of life in an earth that has been adversely affected by sin. Bad things happen because that's life in a sin cursed earth. If you're going to overcome in the challenges of life, you must know that God is not behind your troubles in any way.

WHY DOES GOD ALLOW SUFFERING?

ven if we accept the fact that suffering is in the earth because of Adam and Eve's disobedience, many people still wonder how a good God can allow suffering to remain. We must be clear on what we mean by the word "allow." When people use the phrase "God allows," it's usually loaded with meaning that goes beyond what the Bible teaches. They're often implying that God is in favor of any circumstances—good or bad—occurring in our lives because He let them happen. In our minds, we assume that any event that comes into our lives must have God's approval because if God didn't want it to happen, He would stop it. But it's clear from the Bible that God *does not* stop things from happening even though He's not in favor of them. God "allows" people to sin even though He abhors sin. He "allows" people to go to hell even though 2 Peter 3:9 says God is not willing that any should perish but that all should come to faith in Christ.

There's a common belief among Christians that everything happens for a reason. Implicit in this idea is the assumption that God is ultimately behind everything that takes place. But all sorts of things happen in this life that aren't the will of God. Jesus said some things happen because the devil is trying to steal from you, kill you, and destroy you. Much of the evil in the world is the result of men's sinful choices—going all the way back to Adam. I'm not saying that your current trial is the result of your sin. It may be, but more than likely, it's simply the product of life in a sin cursed earth.

Perhaps you've struggled with thoughts like these: "How can a good God allow a child to be molested and not intervene?" "How can a good God allow innocent people to suffer and not do something about it?" Granted, a lot of mystery surrounds the topic of suffering and at this stage in our existence, none of us can fully explain why every case of suffering occurs. But we can't let what we don't yet understand undermine what the Bible clearly reveals to us about God and His goodness. Consider what we do know about a good God and suffering:

• Suffering is here because of sin, but it won't go on forever. When Jesus returns to earth, all pain and suffering will finally and permanently cease (Revelation 21:4).

• 6,000 to 10,000 years of human history and all the suffering humanity has endured is small in comparison to eternity. No one in heaven today is crying over the hardships they experienced in this life. I am in no way minimizing the suffering people endure. However, a proper perspective on eternity can lighten the load of life's hardships (2 Corinthians 4:17-18).

• When human history on this fallen earth is finally wrapped up, it will be a monument for all eternity as to what happens when men choose independence from God (Genesis 2:17; Romans 6:23).

- God, who is omniscient (all knowing) and omnipotent (all powerful), is able to take evil and suffering, cause it to serve His eternal purposes, and bring great good out of it (Romans 8:28; Ephesians 1:11).

GOD IS SOVEREIGN

Many of the misconceptions about what God is like and how He treats people come from a misunderstanding of God's sovereignty. When people make the statement that "God is sovereign" in response to life's trials, they often mean: "This afflictive circumstance has come from the hand of God and He can do whatever He wants because He knows best." It's not uncommon to hear people say that God can and will make people sick, refuse to heal someone, or take a loved one's life because He is sovereign. But this isn't what sovereign means. The dictionary defines "sovereign" as "the supreme or highest power and authority." To say that "God is sovereign" means He is the Supreme Power in the universe. God is "omni," which means "all." God is omnipotent or all powerful. God is omniscient or all knowing. God is omnipresent or all present (present everywhere at once).

Because God is all powerful and the highest authority in the universe, He is able to cause everything (good and bad) to serve His purposes. Ephesians 1:11 says of God, *"Who works out everything in conformity with the purpose of his will"* (NIV). God doesn't orchestrate afflictive circumstances, but He does use them. His use of suffering and evil is actually a demonstration of His sovereignty. God is so powerful that He is able to take the very real evil that is present in this world because of sin and Satan and bring genuine good out of it.

God doesn't cause everything that happens and He doesn't do everything people attribute to Him. I've had some people ask, "How can this be true? If God is sovereign and all powerful, then isn't He responsible for everything that happens?" The Bible says there are some things God *does not* do and some things He *cannot* do.

- **God does not change.** Malachi 3:6 says: *"For I am the Lord, I change not."* James 1:17 says: *"Every good and perfect gift is from above, coming down from the Father of the heavenly lights, who does not change like shifting shadows"* (NIV). Everything from the hand of God is good and that never changes. "Sovereign" does not mean changeable.

- **God does not violate mankind's free will.** It is not God's will that anyone die and be eternally separated from Him in hell. Yet, people regularly choose independence from God, rejecting His Lordship, and God does not violate their choice. Jesus, who expressed His Father's heart, longed to gather Israel to Himself when He was on this earth, but by an act of their will, they refused. *"O Jerusalem, Jerusalem, you who kill the prophets and stone those sent to you, how often I have longed to gather your children together, as a hen gathers her chicks under her wings, but you were not willing"* (Matthew 23:37, NIV). Jesus, who is God and shows us God, did not violate their choice to reject Him. Yet, as we study scripture, we see that because God is sovereign, He was able to use Israel's rejection of Jesus and cause it to serve His purposes. Through their rejection of the Messiah, the good news of salvation through faith in Christ was taken to the Gentiles.

- **God cannot lie.** He cannot contradict His own Word of truth (Hebrews 6:18; Titus 1:2; John 17:17). God cannot deny Himself. 2 Timothy 2:13 says *"He cannot deny his own nature"* (J.B. Phillips); *"There's no way he can be false to himself"* (The Message). The fact that God cannot deny Himself means He cannot act in a way that is contrary to who He is by nature. And by nature, God is good, which means He cannot act contrary to His goodness. Sovereign does not mean "arbitrary" (impulsive) or "capricious" (fickle).

GOD CAN DO WHATEVER HE WANTS

Most of us have probably heard at some point in our lives that God can do whatever He wants because He's sovereign. Let's think about this statement for a moment. If God is sovereign and can do whatever He wants, then a natural question is "What exactly does He want?" As we study the Bible, we see that God wants a family. God's plan and purpose since before He formed the earth was and is to have a family of sons and daughters who are conformed to the image of Jesus Christ (Ephesians 1:4-5; Romans 8:29). The Bible tells the story of God's desire for a family and the lengths to which He went to obtain His family through the death, burial, and resurrection of Jesus Christ.

It's clear from scripture that God wants relationship with man. We see this theme from Genesis to Revelation. God made man in His image, as much like Himself as a creature can be like his Creator. Why? So relationship would be possible. When God created Adam, He made a son (Luke 3:38). After Adam and Eve sinned in the Garden, God searched for them, not in anger, but with a desire to help them. He offered temporary help through coats of skin to cover their sin (Genesis 3:21) and He offered permanent help—the promise of a Redeemer who

19

would one day remove their sin (Genesis 3:15).

As we read through the Old Testament, we see hints of God's desire for a relationship with man: Enoch was a man who walked with God in a manner that was so pleasing, God took him to heaven without Enoch experiencing physical death (Genesis 5:21-24; Hebrews 11:5). God came down to Abraham to talk with him about Sodom and Gomorrah (Genesis 18:17). Abraham is called the "friend of God" in three places in the Bible (James 2:23; 2 Chronicles 20:7; Isaiah 41:8). God also spoke to Moses as a man speaks to his friend (Exodus 33:11).

In the New Testament, Jesus—who is God and shows us God—told His disciples, *"Ye are my friends, if ye do whatsoever I command you"* (John 15:14). He also said, *"Whosoever shall do the will of my Father which is in heaven, the same is my brother, and sister, and mother"* (Matthew 12:50).

The Bible says that when sin and its effects have been removed from God's creation following the return of Jesus to this earth, we'll continue to see relationship between God and man. *"Then I saw a new earth...and a new sky, for the present earth and sky had disappeared. And I, John, saw the Holy City, the new Jerusalem, coming down from God out of heaven. It was a glorious sight, beautiful as a bride at her wedding. I heard a loud shout from the throne saying, "Look, the home of God is now among men, and he will live with them and they will be his people; yes, God himself will be among them. He will wipe away all tears from their eyes, and there shall be no more death, nor sorrow, nor crying, nor pain. All of that has gone forever." And the one sitting on the throne said...Everyone who conquers will inherit all these blessings, and I will be his God and he will be my son"* (Revelation 21:1-5,7, TLB).

The prophet Isaiah also describes this time in his writings. We see from Isaiah's prophecy that God is working toward a party with His sons and daughters. *"Here on Mount Zion in Jerusalem, the Lord of Hosts will spread a wondrous feast for everyone around the world—a delicious feast of good food, with clear, well-aged wine and choice beef. At that time he will remove the cloud of gloom, the pall of death that hangs over the earth; he will swallow up death forever. The Lord God will wipe away all tears and take away forever all insults and mockery against his land and people. The Lord has spoken—he will surely do it!"* (Isaiah 25:6-8, TLB).

God wants to draw all men to Himself so He can have a family. As an expression of His wisdom, power, and kindness, God sent Jesus to die for our sins. God, in His sovereignty, has helped mankind with our greatest need—salvation from our sins—through the death, burial, and resurrection of Jesus Christ. *"But because of his great love for us, God, who is rich in mercy, made us alive with Christ even when we were dead in transgressions—it is by grace you have been saved. And God raised us up with Christ and seated us with him in the heavenly realms in Christ Jesus, in order that in the coming ages he might show the incomparable riches of his grace, expressed in his kindness to us in Christ Jesus"* (Ephesians 2:4-7, NIV).

God wants relationship with man and He's making a family for Himself. Because He's sovereign, He can cause everything to serve this purpose—even things He is not responsible for. In the context of God making us His sons through faith in Christ, Ephesians 1:9-11 says, *"For God has allowed us to know the secret of his plan, and it is this: he purposed long ago in his sovereign will that all human history should be consummated in Christ, that everything that exists in Heaven or earth should find its perfection and fulfillment in him. In Christ we have been given an inheritance, since we were destined for this, by the One who works out all his purposes according to the designs of his own will"* (J.B. Phillips).

The Cross was a mighty display of God's sovereignty. God, in His omniscience (all knowingness), knew that the devil would inspire evil men to crucify the innocent Son of God (Luke 22:3; Acts 2:23). God used their wicked act to bring about the greatest good ever accomplished in the history of the universe. Jesus took the sins of men on Himself and purchased the salvation of the human race. Through the Cross of Christ, God obtained His family. 1 Corinthians 2:8 says that had the devil known what God was going to do through the Cross, he never would have crucified the Lord of Glory.

Not only was the Cross a demonstration of God's omniscience, it was a tremendous display of His omnipotence (His power). The resurrection of Jesus was opposed by all the powers of darkness. Because of that tremendous opposition, His resurrection involved the greatest display ever of God's power as God triumphed over sin, Satan, and death (Ephesians 1:19; Colossians 2:15). God beat the devil at his own game because God is sovereign.

Some say that because God is sovereign He can do bad to people because He knows what's best for them in the long run. But the opposite is true. God uses His sovereignty to bless and be kind to people, not to harm them. He uses His sovereignty to demonstrate His grace and goodness toward mankind. According to the Bible, God, as the Sovereign Lord of the universe, has the right to display His kindness as He chooses. *"For God had said to Moses, 'If I want to be kind to someone, I will. And I will take pity on anyone I want to '"* (Romans 9:15, TLB). Right now, God, who is all powerful and the highest authority, is causing everything—including human choices—to serve His purposes in order to bring maximum glory to Himself and maximum good to as many people as possible as He gathers His family.

GOD IS THE POTTER

One reason for confusion over where troubles come from is that people misapply scriptures about God's sovereignty. A prime example is found in Romans 9:20-22: *"But who are you, O man, to talk back to God? Shall what is formed say to him who formed it, 'Why did you make me like this?' Does not the potter have the right to make out of the same lump of clay some pottery for noble purposes and some for common use? What if God, choosing to show his wrath and make his power known, bore with great patience the objects of his wrath— prepared for destruction?"* (NIV). Based on these scriptures, people often make statements like this: "God can give us a car wreck or cancer to mold us. We don't have the right to question His sovereignty because He is the Potter and we are the clay. He can do whatever He wants to do." Drawing this conclusion from the verses in Romans 9 is a direct result of not letting scripture define scripture. To accurately interpret these verses, we must determine what the author, the Apostle Paul, meant when he called God the Potter.

God is referred to as a Potter only a few times in scripture (Isaiah 29:15-16; 45:9; 64:8; Jeremiah 18:1-10). In each instance, God is addressing *nations*, not *individuals*. These passages describe God as a Potter to reflect His interaction with the nation of Israel when they rebelled against Him and worshipped false gods. These scriptures explain the consequences of Israel's rejection of God, indicating that God the Potter had the right to let Israel's enemies overrun them if they persisted in idol worship.

23

The verses *don't* refer to individuals suffering hardship, loss, or disease for vague reasons known only to the sovereign God.

The sole New Testament reference to God as the Potter is found in Romans 9:20-22 and it is actually a quote from Jeremiah 18. Paul uses the quote to support his position that God has not been unfair in giving the gospel to the Gentiles in light of Israel's rejection of Christ as their Messiah.

The subject under discussion in Romans 9 is God's dealings with the nation of Israel—not His dealings with individuals on a daily basis. These verses are not an explanation of the evil and suffering in our personal lives. In context, the picture of God as the Potter who molds clay vessels refers to God's choice of Israel as His special people in the Old Testament and His choice of the Church in the New Testament. Paul's point is that God's choice of Israel and the Church is fair and just because, as the sovereign God, He has the right to demonstrate His kindness to whomever He wishes (Romans 9:15). (See Note 3 for a more detailed discussion on Romans 9 and God's sovereignty.)

Is it wrong to say that God is the Potter and we are the clay? No, as long as you understand these key points. Yes, God is the Potter and we are the clay, but as we've seen, this doesn't mean God can or will do bad to you because He is sovereign. God does shape us. But He shapes us inwardly by His Word and His Spirit. *"And all of us, as with unveiled face, [because we] continued to behold [in the Word of God] as in a mirror the glory of the Lord, are constantly being transfigured into His very own image in ever increasing splendor and from one degree of glory to another; [for this comes] from the Lord [Who is] the Spirit"* (2 Corinthians 3:18, AMP). God the Potter is also God your Father and He will mold you and shape you as a Father—with love. *"But now, O Lord, thou art our father; we are the clay, and thou our potter; and we all are the work of thy hand"* (Isaiah 64:8).

· →→→→ · ←←←← ·

Evil and suffering are present in the world because of sin, beginning with Adam's sin. But it will not go on forever. God, in His sovereignty, is able to take genuine evil and bring genuine good out of it. In His wisdom and power, He's able to beat the devil at his own game and cause everything to serve His purposes. God's desire is to bring maximum glory to Himself and maximum good to as many people as possible as He gathers His family.

Now that we've laid a strong foundation for the fact that God is good and good means good, let's deal with some of the common "Yes, but what about…?" questions.

YES, BUT WHAT ABOUT THE OLD TESTAMENT?

*O*ne of the first questions I've heard people raise in response to what I've said so far is: "If God is a good God and good means good, then how do you explain God's actions in the Old Testament? What about all the places where God killed people, made people sick, and punished people with destruction?" We can't address every incident in the Old Testament in this short book, but we can cover a few principles that will answer our first "Yes, but what about…?" question and give us guidelines to help us as we read the Old Testament.

God's goodness, mercy, and love are found throughout the Old Testament. The word "mercy" appears 261 times in the King James Bible. Seventy-two percent of those times, the word is found in the Old Testament. The word "love" appears 322 times in the King James Bible and almost half of those times are in the Old Testament. However, we do have to look a little closer to see God's mercy and love in the Old Testament. The Bible is progressive revelation, which means that God has gradually revealed Himself to mankind through the pages of scripture. Many things are not fully stated in the Old Testament. God's goodness, mercy, and love aren't always as clearly spelled out in the Old Testament as they are in the New Testament.

In the Old Testament, we do not yet have the complete picture of God that is revealed to us through Jesus Christ in the New Testament. Hebrews 1:3 says Jesus is the *express image* of God. The word "express" comes from a word meaning an "impression made by a stamp." Jesus is the exact representation of the Father. As I noted earlier, if you want to know how God treats people, look at Jesus. We don't start our study of God with the Old Testament. We start with the New Testament. We start with what Jesus shows us about God. Once we have a clear image of God as He is revealed in Jesus in the New Testament, we filter the Old Testament through that picture.

To filter the Old Testament through the New Testament means two primary things. First, it means that if you have 10 verses from the New Testament that clearly support an idea or theme and one verse from the Old Testament that seems to contradict those 10 verses, you don't throw out the 10 New Testament verses. The Bible doesn't contradict itself. The fact that a verse seems to contradict other scriptures means you don't yet have full understanding of that verse. Put aside the verse that seems to contradict until you have a better grasp of it. Second, to filter the Old Testament through the New Testament means we must find out what the New Testament says about specific events in the Old Testament. For example, the Book of Job scares a lot of people. But the New Testament tells us what we should get out of reading the Book of Job. According to James 5:11, Job teaches us that God is a merciful God who delivers His people from bondage. If you don't get that picture of God from the Book of Job, you haven't read the book in its proper context. We'll review Job more fully in the next chapter.

KEYS TO READING THE OLD TESTAMENT

Understanding Context

To rightly understand the Old Testament, we must learn to read in context. Everything in the Bible was written by someone to someone about something. Whenever we read the Bible, we have to determine who's speaking, who's receiving the message, and the topic under discussion in order to accurately interpret the meaning of a verse. By saying that the Bible was written by someone to someone about something, I don't mean that the Bible is the word of men rather than the Word of God. I simply mean that God inspired certain men to write to other men about particular issues. For example, God used the Apostle Paul to write two letters to a man named Timothy in order to instruct Timothy on how to pastor the churches he oversaw. You must know that information to get full understanding of those two epistles.

Another important key to reading the Old Testament is understanding the historical and cultural context in which it was written. The Old Testament deals primarily with the history of Israel. Much of the nation's history is sad and dark because the Israelites repeatedly worshipped the idols and false gods of the people who lived around them and took on their immoral lifestyles and practices. At various times in Israel's history, the Hebrews committed many gross sins. They worshipped idols in God's Temple in Jerusalem (Ezekiel 8), sacrificed their sons and daughters to idols by burning them alive (Psalm 106:37-38), and acknowledged idols made of wood and stone as their creator instead of God (Jeremiah 2:27). God sent prophets to Israel, warning the Hebrews of coming destruction at the hands of their enemies if they did not repent. Israel rejected God's warnings and, as a result, experienced the consequences of their horrific sins.

Because of a lack of understanding about context, people often take Old Testament verses that were written to an idol-worshipping nation and apply them to present-day believers who occasionally fall short when faced with life's everyday challenges. As a result, many Christians live in unnecessary fear of punishment from God based on verses that have been misapplied.

Understanding Language

We must also understand that when the Old Testament makes statements such as "God brought sickness among the people," it did not mean to the original readers what it means to us today. The Old Testament was originally written in Hebrew. It was a common Hebrew idiom to use a causative verb when a permissive sense was intended. God was said to do (causative) what He in fact only allowed (permissive). Even though the text literally says "God *sent* sickness among the people," the Israelites would have understood it to mean "God *allowed* sickness among the people." (See Note 4 for more information.)

How can we tell whether an Old Testament verse means "God did" or "God allowed" if we don't know the Hebrew language? Sometimes the meaning is obvious from the passage itself. 1 Chronicles 10:14 says the Lord killed King Saul. But if we read the entire chapter, we find that Saul asked his armor bearer to kill him. When the man refused, Saul fell on his own sword and killed himself. The Lord didn't kill Saul. The Lord allowed Saul to kill himself. In Exodus 15:26 God said to Israel, if they would keep His commandments, "*I will put none of these diseases upon thee, which I have brought upon the Egyptians: for I am the Lord that healeth thee.*" The proper interpretation of this scripture would be "I will allow none of the diseases of Egypt to come on you." The phrase "the Lord that healeth thee" is Jehovah Rapha in the Hebrew, which means "the Lord your Physician." God does not make people sick only to turn around and make them well. That would be a house divided against itself. (Remember what Jesus said in Matthew 12:24-26 about a house divided.) When we can't tell from the passage itself if God "did" or God "allowed," we must assess the verse in terms of the New Testament. If what the verse says God "did" is contrary to the revelation of God given to us by Jesus Christ in the New Testament, then we know the verse must be understood to mean that God "allowed."

THE ONLY GOD, GOD ALMIGHTY

When God brought Israel out of bondage in Egypt under the leadership of Moses, the entire world was polytheistic (worshipped many gods). Only Israel was monotheistic (worshipped one God), and that, just barely. A number of the Hebrew people fell into idol worship in Egypt and then returned to it in the wilderness on the way to the Promised Land (Ezekiel 20:6-10; Exodus 32:1-6). When Israel finally entered the land of Canaan, they repeatedly slipped back into worshipping false gods.

Most of the nations surrounding Israel had a god of light, a god of dark, a god of day, a god of night, a god of good, and a god of evil, among many others. One of God's primary purposes in the Old Testament was to reveal Himself to His people and to the nations around Israel as God Almighty—the Only, All-Powerful God. That is one reason why we see so many fierce demonstrations of His power in the Old Testament.

The writers of the Old Testament, under the inspiration of the Holy Spirit, connected many destructive events with God. They didn't do this because God was behind the destruction, but to help Israel understand that calamity came—not because the fire god was angry or the harvest god needed to be appeased— but because they were out of right relationship with Almighty God due to their idol worship. God's goal was to build into human consciousness the idea that His people must be in right relationship with Him, the Only, All-Powerful God, first through the Law and its sacrifices, and ultimately through Jesus Christ.

The Bible states that God is good and God is love. However, those themes are not as prominent in the Old Testament. If God had clearly revealed Himself as a loving Father in a world that worshipped many gods, Israel and the surrounding nations may have mistakenly viewed God as the "love God"—just one more god among many gods. There is very little mention of the Triune God (Father, Son, and Holy Spirit) in the Old Testament for the same reason.

Let's look at a few examples of how understanding the historical context of the Old Testament can help us explain a verse that appears to attribute bad or evil to God. In Exodus 20:5 God says: *"Thou shalt not bow down thyself to them* (idols)*, nor serve them: for I the Lord thy God am a jealous God, visiting the iniquity of the fathers upon the children unto the third and fourth generation of them that hate me."* I've had people quote this verse to me as proof that God does bad to people. "After all," they say, "God visits the sins of the fathers on the sons." But remember, we always have to read scriptures in context. God spoke these words to Moses while Israel was on their way to the Promised Land. God had just given Moses the first part of the Ten Commandments: Israel was not to have any other gods and was not to make or bow down to idols. Then God made the statement about children being punished for the sins of their fathers.

Just before Israel actually entered the land of Canaan, God warned them that if they worshipped the gods of the people of Canaan, He would allow their enemies to overrun them and take them out of the land (Deuteronomy 4:25-28). Israel did not obey God. They repeatedly worshipped the gods of the nations around them, and, as God had warned, they were overrun and scattered by their enemies—first Assyria and then Babylon. In 586 B.C., the Babylonians took Israel into captivity where they remained for 70 years. What God declared in Exodus 20:5 came to pass. Israel was carted off to Babylon because of the sins of the fathers (Israel's repeated idol worship). As a result, their children were born in Babylon and had to live in bondage for 70 years, down to the third and fourth generations—down to the time of the grandchildren and the great grandchildren. God's statement in Exodus 20:5 was not a declaration of His plans to punish people for their sins by punishing their offspring down to the fourth generation. He simply warned Israel of the consequences they would experience if they worshipped idols in the Promised Land.

In Isaiah 45:7, God says, "*I form the light, and create darkness: I make peace, and create evil: I the Lord do all these things.*" Many people read this verse and think: "See! God does do evil to people. After all, He is sovereign and He knows best." Again, knowing the historical context is vital to understanding what God is saying in this verse. Persia, under the rulership of King Cyrus the Great, conquered the Babylonian Empire in 539 B.C. The next year, King Cyrus allowed the Hebrew people who had been held captive in Babylon for 70 years to return to their homeland. Cyrus' rise to power and his decision to permit Israel to go back to Canaan was fulfillment of a prophecy recorded in the Book of Isaiah. Through the prophet Isaiah, 150 years before Cyrus was born, God identified the king by name as the instrument through which He would bring His people back to the Promised Land (Isaiah 44:28–45:4).

The prophecy is followed by a lengthy passage where God clearly states that there is no God but Him. Speaking to King Cyrus, God says, *"I am the Lord; there is no other God. I have prepared you, even though you do not know me, so all the world from east to west will know there is no other God. I am the Lord, and there is no other"* (Isaiah 45:5-6, NLT). Then comes the statement in verse 7, *"I form the light, and create darkness: I make peace, and create evil: I the Lord do all these things."* God is still talking to King Cyrus. Cyrus and the Persians believed in a god of good and a god of evil. The good god was the god of light and the evil god was the god of darkness.

By His statement in verse 7, God is making it clear to Cyrus, "There are no gods of light and dark, good and evil. I am ultimately in control of everything—light, dark, good, evil, you—because I am God Almighty. There is no other god." The fact that God is ultimately in control of everything does not mean He causes or approves of everything that happens. It means that nothing takes Him by surprise and nothing happens that He cannot cause to serve His purposes.

In this passage, God is not saying He does bad to people. He is declaring His omnipotence to Cyrus and the Persians so that they will turn from their false gods and acknowledge Him as the only God. Just a few verses later God says: *"And there is no God apart from me, a righteous God and a Saviour; there is none but me. Turn to me and be saved, all you ends of the earth; for I am God, and there is no other"* (Isaiah 45:21-22, NIV). When we consider Isaiah 45:7 in its historical context, we see that it is not a declaration of the fact that God might bring calamity into your life for some sovereign purpose. Rather, it is a statement of God's goodness as He seeks to draw Cyrus and the Persians to Himself by showing them that He alone is God.

A GOOD GOD AND PLAGUES

Another common question I receive is: "How could a good God send plagues on the Egyptians?" The nation of Egypt held Israel in captivity for 400 years. Near the end of this period of bondage, a man named Moses, under the direction of God, went to Pharaoh with a message from the Lord: "Let my people go so they may serve me." Pharaoh refused and the Egyptians experienced a series of plagues that were said to come from God.

Each plague was actually a demonstration of God's power and a challenge to the Egyptian gods. For example, the Egyptians considered the Nile River to be their source of life. Every year, they sacrificed a boy and a girl to the Nile. By turning the waters of the Nile to blood, God demonstrated the fact that He is greater than the Nile—He is the source of life; He created the Nile; He controls the Nile. The Egyptian goddess Heket was depicted as a frog. Through the plague of frogs, God showed the Egyptians that frogs are not gods. He showed them that He—the Only, All-Powerful God—controls the frogs. The plagues were designed to show the Egyptians that their idols were not gods at all. They were designed to show the Egyptians that God is the true God, the only God, so that the Egyptians would come to faith in Him.

35

The plagues occurred over a nine-month period. Up until the last one, the plagues were annoyances, but not deadly. As a group, the Egyptians could have avoided these displays of power if Pharaoh had released Israel from bondage. And as individuals, the Egyptians could have joined Israel to avoid the calamities because Israel—the people of the Only, All-Powerful God—was not affected by the plagues (Exodus 8:22-23; 9:4,26).

These power demonstrations had their desired effect. Through the plagues, many Egyptians acknowledged that the Hebrew God, Jehovah, was the one true God (Exodus 8:19; 9:19-21). Scripture tells us that when Israel finally left Egypt, a "mixed multitude" went with them (Exodus 12:38). In that mix were Egyptians who had come to believe on God.

What about the final plague, the death of the firstborn of the Egyptians, including men and animals? Exodus 12:12 says, *"For I will pass through the land of Egypt this night, and will smite all the firstborn in the land of Egypt, both man and beast; and against all the gods of Egypt I will execute judgment: I am the Lord."* How could a good God do that? Consider these points:

- The night the deaths were supposed to occur, God told His people to put the blood of a lamb on their doorposts and they would be protected. *"For the Lord will pass through to smite the Egyptians; and when he seeth the blood upon the lintel, and on the two side posts, the Lord will pass over the door, and will not suffer the destroyer to come in unto your houses to smite you"* (Exodus 12:23). God did not kill the Egyptians. How do we know that? First, such an action is a complete contradiction of the revelation of God given to us through Jesus Christ. Second, Exodus 12:23 says the destruction was carried out by the destroyer. Jesus identified Satan as the one who kills and destroys. The New Testament says that it is Satan who *"holds the power of death"* (Hebrews 2:14, NIV).

- Earlier, God told Pharaoh it was His sovereign kindness that had kept Pharaoh and the Egyptians from being destroyed by the destroyer in the past. *"For by now I could have put forth My hand and have struck you and your people with pestilence, and you would have been cut off from the earth. But for this very purpose have I let you live, that I might show you My power, and that My name may be declared throughout all the earth"* (Exodus 9:15-16, AMP). The original Hebrew language for "I have let you live" says, "I have caused thee to stand." Up to this point, God had preserved the Egyptians from being destroyed by past calamities so that He could have a further chance to show them that He, Jehovah, is the only true God. Yet, Egypt repeatedly rejected God's kindness throughout the duration of His power demonstrations. That night, God permitted the Egyptians to reap the fruit of their rejection of Him, and the destroyer destroyed all their firstborn.

- The first time Moses spoke to Pharaoh, Moses warned him that if he did not free Israel, Egypt's firstborn sons would die (Exodus 4:22-23). During the next nine months, everything Moses said would happen came to pass. Pharaoh had all that time to heed Moses' initial warning, including another visit from Moses with a final warning just before the last plague came upon Egypt (Exodus 11:4-7). No one had to die that night.

GOD'S PURPOSES ARE REDEMPTIVE

God's purposes are always redemptive. That means His goal is to *save* as many people as possible, not to *destroy* as many people as possible. Let's look at God's redemptive nature in the light of Noah and the flood. During the time that Noah lived, there was great wickedness in the earth. The Bible says that only Noah served the Lord. In response, God decided to destroy the entire population of the earth. How could a good God do such a thing?

To answer that question, we have to look back at something that happened in the Garden of Eden shortly after Adam and Eve sinned. At that time, God promised them that He would send Jesus to undo the damage caused by their sin. God said to the serpent (Satan), *"And I will put enmity between thee and the woman, and between thy seed and her seed* (Jesus)*; it shall bruise thy head, and thou shalt bruise his heel"* (Genesis 3:15). This is the first reference in the Bible to the Lord Jesus Christ and His death on the Cross. Notice that God spoke of *the* woman from whom the seed would come (Mary). God had already marked out the family line through which the Redeemer of mankind would ultimately be born. Luke 3:38 tells us that the righteous line from which Jesus would come was to proceed through Seth, the third son of Adam and Eve.

By the time of Noah, the descendants of Seth were in danger of being wiped out by sin. They were intermarrying with Cain's descendants and were being corrupted. (Cain, Adam's firstborn, had murdered Abel, Adam's second born.) Only Noah, a descendent of Seth, and his family, continued to serve God. If Seth's entire family line were destroyed by sin and corruption, then God's promise of a seed (Jesus Christ) who would bruise the head of the serpent (break his power) would not have been fulfilled. God had to preserve the righteous line through which the Redeemer would come, which meant He had to rid the earth of the corruption that could have ultimately influenced Noah, the only remaining righteous man in Seth's family line.

Many people who read about the flood have an image of an angry, volatile God who, out of frustration, decided to wipe out mankind. But God was sorry it had come to this. He did not create man for this pitiful state. *"When the Lord God saw the extent of human wickedness, and that the trend and direction of men's lives were only towards evil, he was sorry he had made them. It broke his heart"* (Genesis 6:5-6, TLB).

When we look closely at the account of the flood we see the great patience of God. He gave the entire population of the world 120 years to come back to Him. *"My Spirit must not forever be disgraced in man, wholly evil as he is. I will give him 120 years to mend his ways"* (Genesis 6:3, TLB). During that time, God worked to draw men to repentance by sending prophets to plead with them and to warn them to turn from sin back toward Him. A prophet named Enoch preached during this period about the coming of the Lord to earth to deal with sin (Jude 14). Enoch named his son Methuselah, which means "after him, the flood," a further warning of what was ahead if people did not repent. Methuselah lived 969 years, longer than anyone else in the Bible, which demonstrated God's willingness to give men ample opportunity to turn from wickedness to Him.

People saw Noah working on the ark for 120 years and during that entire period, Noah preached to them about being in right relationship with God (2 Peter 2:5). There were people on earth during Noah's lifetime who actually knew Adam and Eve. Methuselah, Noah's grandfather, was alive during the last

243 years of Adam's life. Noah's father, Lamech, was alive during the last 50 years of Adam's life. Adam's grandson, Enos, died when Noah was 98. All of these people could have heard Adam talk about God and the Garden of Eden. That means the people living prior to the flood had the testimony of two human beings, Adam and Eve, who had actually walked with God on earth. A careful study of the flood shows us that God's purposes were redemptive. God endeavored to save as many people as possible.

RAHAB'S REDEMPTION

Let's look at another spectacular example of God's redemptive purposes, this time in the midst of the destruction of the city of Jericho. Jericho was the first city the Israelites reached when they entered the Promised Land. Before Israel attacked Jericho, Joshua, the Hebrews' new leader, sent two spies into the city to examine the land. Someone informed the King of Jericho that the men were in the city. God used Rahab, an idol-worshipping prostitute, to hide the spies and help them escape.

As the Hebrew spies talked with Rahab she explained why she was willing to help them. *"I know that the Lord has given this land to you and that a great fear of you has fallen on us, so that all who live in this country are melting in fear because of you. We have heard how the Lord dried up the water of the Red Sea for you when you came out of Egypt...When we heard of it, our hearts sank and everyone's courage failed because of you, for the Lord your God is God in heaven above and on the earth below"* (Joshua 2:9-11, NIV). Rahab spoke these words 40 years after God had delivered Israel from bondage in Egypt, making a way of escape for them by parting the Red Sea.

As you may recall, the generation of people who originally came out of Egypt refused to enter the Promised Land and wandered in the wilderness for 40 years. At the end of that time, Joshua led the next generation of Israelites into the Promised Land. Forty years later, people were still talking about what God did to Egypt and people like Rahab were acknowledging Jehovah as God Almighty. God's power demonstrations in Egypt had their desired effect. They showed the heathen world that He alone is God.

Rahab appealed to the spies for mercy. They agreed to protect her and gave her a red cord to hang in her window. The spies promised Rahab that her house and anyone in the house with her would be spared when the Israelites took over Jericho. True to their word, the Israelites spared Rahab and her family (Joshua 2:18-21; 6:22-23). You might ask: "Why were Rahab and her family the only ones saved? What about the other people in the city of Jericho?" Consider this point: Israel marched around Jericho for seven days prior to the destruction of the city. Anyone could have come out of the city and asked for mercy from Jehovah. Anyone inside the city could have asked Him for mercy. God always receives those who come to Him in true repentance and faith.

A FINAL THOUGHT

As I said at the beginning of this chapter, we can't address every troubling incident in the Old Testament in this short book. But we have covered a few principles to help you understand the Old Testament more fully:

- Context and historical background are crucial to proper understanding.

- When a verse says "God did," the original readers understood it to mean "God allowed."

- One of God's primary goals in the Old Testament was to show an idol-worshipping world that He is the Only God, God Almighty.

If you come to a troubling incident in the Old Testament, don't throw out everything you know about God's goodness as revealed in Jesus. It's better to presume that you don't yet have full understanding of that particular Old Testament event. Ask the Holy Spirit to help you understand the passage in light of the entire Bible and in light of God's goodness. God's purposes are always redemptive. The God revealed to us in the Old Testament is the same God revealed to us in the New Testament. There is no contradiction. It's simply a matter of learning how to read the Old Testament. God is a good God... and good means good...in both the Old and New Testaments.

YES, BUT WHAT ABOUT JOB?

"*Y*es, but what about Job?" is another common question I receive from people when they hear that God does not harm His children. People want to know: "If God is good and good means good, then how do you explain what happened to Job?" They go on to say: "God may not have directly touched Job, but it's clear that He commissioned the devil to attack Job. But the Book of Job *cannot* say that God afflicted Job either directly or indirectly because that is contrary to the way Jesus treated men when He was on this earth. How do we resolve this seeming contradiction?

Because the Book of Job is located in the Old Testament, we need to use some of the principles mentioned in the previous chapter: We must read Job in the light of the New Testament and what Jesus shows us about God. We must consider who wrote Job, why the writer wrote the book, and to whom he wrote. If we utilize these principles, we will see that Job does not contradict the fact that God is good and good means good. Actually, the book clearly demonstrates the goodness of God.

Let's briefly summarize Job's story. At the beginning of the book, Job is introduced as a perfect, upright man who feared God and avoided evil. He had a large family and great material wealth. After a short description of Job and his children, the Bible records two conversations between God and Satan about Job. Subsequent to those conversations, Satan destroyed Job's wealth and his children and gave him a terrible skin disease. The text tells us that Satan's goal was to prove that Job only served God because of the good things in his life and that if those things were taken away, Job would renounce God.

Three of Job's friends came to comfort him. Most of the book is a dialogue between Job and his friends as they try to figure out why all this evil happened to Job. His comforters assumed he must have sinned terribly to be so afflicted. Job insisted he had done nothing wrong to deserve such tragedies. Finally, a man named Elihu came on the scene and talked about God's justice and mercy. Then, God Himself spoke to Job from a whirlwind and reprimanded him and his friends. In the end, Job repented for speaking foolishly about things he did not understand, prayed for his friends, and saw God restore to him twice as much as he had before his troubles began.

THE PURPOSE OF JOB

People misunderstand the purpose of the Book of Job and, as a result, misinterpret Job's story. The standard interpretation of Job is that it was written to explain why there is so much undeserved suffering in life. People conclude that God and Satan are at work behind the scenes—that God sometimes permits the devil to afflict men for sovereign purposes and we must trust His wisdom. But Job was not written to explain why people suffer. Job and his three friends all speculated as to why Job was suffering. Job himself asked "why" at least 20 times. All the men were wrong in their conclusions and all were rebuked by God. The book does not address why troubles came into Job's life beyond the general information that Satan was the source of his sufferings.

What *is* the purpose of the Book of Job? To answer that question, we must determine what Job would have meant to the people to whom it was first written. Remember, everything in the Bible was written by someone to someone about something. The Book of Job cannot mean something to us that it would not have meant to the people who first heard his story.

Most Bible scholars believe that Job is the earliest book of the Bible. It was written by Moses during the 40 years he lived in the deserts of Midian, where he fled after he killed an Egyptian prior to leading Israel out of Egypt. Midian was adjacent to the land of Uz, Job's home. Although the events of Job's story took place well before Moses lived (probably during the time of Abraham), Moses heard Job's story and, under the inspiration of the Holy Spirit, transcribed it. When Moses wrote the Book of Job, the Israelites were in slavery in Egypt, having been in bondage for more than 400 years with no seeming way out. Moses recorded Job's story to give Israel hope by encouraging them that God delivers men who are suffering under afflictive bondage.

That interpretation is consistent with the New Testament. According to Romans 15:4, the Old Testament was written, in part, to give men hope or expectation of coming good. *"For all those words which were written long ago are meant to teach us today; so that we may be encouraged to endure and to go on hoping in our own time"* (J.B. Phillips). James 5:11, the only New Testament verse that mentions Job directly, commends Job's patience and draws our attention to the end of his story:

"You have heard of Job's patient endurance and how the Lord dealt with him in the end, and therefore you have seen that the Lord is merciful and full of understanding pity" (J.B. Phillips). We read Job and ask, "Why did it happen?" But the Holy Spirit, through James, focuses on how Job's story turned out. *"And the Lord turned the captivity of Job, when he prayed for his friends: also the Lord gave Job twice as much as he had before"* (Job 42:10). In Job, God delivered from bondage a man who stayed true to Him, despite his grievous circumstances. God's earliest written revelation to His people was intended to impart hope by showing them God's goodness and kindness in rescuing faithful Job.

The Book of Job was also written to reveal to Israel that there is an Adversary at work in the earth who challenges God as he works to entice men into rebellion against God. The name Satan is mentioned 19 times in the Old Testament. Fourteen of those times are in the Book of Job. Interestingly, God is called the "Almighty" or Shaddai 31 times in Job, more than all the other times in the Old Testament combined. Shaddai means "mighty" and emphasizes God's power or sovereignty. Some mistakenly say Job's circumstances demonstrate that because God is sovereign, He occasionally uses the devil to afflict people for special purposes. However, that interpretation is not accurate because that is not how the people who first heard Job would have understood its message.

Consider the context in which the Book of Job would have been received by Israel. Until the time of the writing of Job, God's revelations to His people came through direct revelation and oral traditions passed down from one generation to the next. When God initially led Abraham to Canaan, He spoke directly to Abraham, promising the land to him and his descendants. God told Abraham, *"Know for certain that your descendants*

will be strangers in a country not their own, and they will be
enslaved and mistreated four hundred years. But I will punish
the nation they serve as slaves, and afterward they will come
out with great possessions" (Genesis 15:13-14, NIV). Abraham
passed those words on to his children. Many years later, when
Abraham's grandson, Jacob, went to live in Egypt with his
family, God told Jacob He would bring him back to the land of
Canaan (Genesis 46:2-4). Jacob shared that message with his
son Joseph who instructed his sons to take his bones with them
when they went home to Canaan (Genesis 48:21; 50:24-26).
However, after Joseph's death, Egypt enslaved Israel. As the
years of their enslavement dragged on, the Hebrews must have
wondered why they ended up in slavery and if they would ever
be free to return to their land as God had promised Abraham.
Job's story revealed that there is an Adversary who does take
men captive. In Israel's case, idol-worshipping, Satan-inspired
heathen moved by jealousy and fear had enslaved them. But his
story would have encouraged them that God had a plan in mind
to deliver them just as He delivered Job.

The purpose of this revelation about God's power and the
devil's work was not to tell Israel that God sometimes uses the
devil to afflict His people for reasons known only to Him, but
rather to reassure Israel, "Satan cannot do anything that takes
Me by surprise and he cannot do anything that is too big for
Me to handle. No matter what comes your way because of the
work of Satan, I will deliver you from the bondage to which
you have been subjected and I will restore to you what you have
lost." That's how Israel would have understood God's message
in Job.

The Book of Job demonstrates God's sovereignty, not because
He "allowed" the devil to afflict Job, but because He conquered
all the evil that came against Job. The devil's biggest guns—

theft, destruction, and death (all of which are part of life in a sin cursed earth)—were reversed in Job's situation by the hand of God. That's how the original readers would have interpreted Job's story.

JOB: A STORY OF REDEMPTION

The Bible is not a collection of independent, unrelated verses. It is a book with a theme: God's desire for a family and the lengths to which He went to obtain that family through Jesus. Everything in the Bible, including the Book of Job, fits with and contributes to advancing that story line. To properly interpret Job and what it shows us about God, we must consider the book in terms of its connection with the theme of the Bible.

The Bible opens with God creating the earth as a home for His family. When God made Adam, He made a son and a race of sons in Adam (Isaiah 45:18; Luke 3:38; Genesis 5:1). When Adam sinned, mankind and the earth itself went into captivity to sin, death, and Satan. But God immediately promised the coming of One (Jesus Christ) who would undo the damage done by Adam's sin and redeem or deliver men from bondage so that God could have His family back (Genesis 3:15). This promise of redemption was passed down orally until Moses wrote it down in what would become the Old Testament during Israel's 40 years of wilderness wanderings.

In the Old Testament, God repeatedly stated His promise of a Redeemer who would deliver men from enslavement to sin and its consequences. Events and people in the Old Testament foreshadow both the person of Christ (Redeemer) and the work of Christ (redemption). God's deliverance of Israel from captivity in Egypt to bring them into the blessings of the Promised Land is repeatedly referred to in scripture as "redemption" because it pictures our redemption in Christ (Exodus 6:6; 15:13; Psalm 106:10).

Job fits with the Bible's theme of redemption because it is a "mini" story of redemption: God delivered, or redeemed, a man who was captive to the works of the devil. Job also advances the storyline of coming redemption. The Book of Job is the first place in the Bible where the name Redeemer is mentioned: "*I know that my Redeemer lives, and that in the end he will stand upon the earth. And after my skin has been destroyed, yet in my flesh I will see God*" (Job 19:25-26, NIV).

Throughout much of the book, Job maintained that he had done nothing to deserve the calamities that had devastated his life. Although Job repeatedly justified himself, he was aware of his powerlessness with sin and its resulting destruction. Job cried out for someone to remedy his sin. In doing so, Job pictured Jesus and His work of redemption. Consider these verses.

- *"What have I done to you, O watcher of all humanity? Why have you made me your target? ...Why not just pardon my sin and take away my guilt?"* (Job 7:20-21, NLT).

- *"But how can a person be declared innocent in the eyes of God? If only there were a mediator who could bring us together, but there is none. The mediator could make God stop beating me, and I would no longer live in terror of his punishment. Then I could speak to him without fear, but I cannot do that in my own strength"* (Job 9:2,33-35, NLT).

- *"Even now my witness is in heaven; my advocate is on high. My intercessor is my friend as my eyes pour out tears to God; on behalf of a man he pleads with God as a man pleads for his friend"* (Job 16:19-21, NIV).

Job didn't understand that God was not behind his suffering, but he did recognize his helplessness as a sinner before a holy God. Job knew he had no access to God because of his sin. In his cry for help, Job foreshadowed Jesus who is the mediator between God and man. Jesus went to the Cross to take the punishment for sin, remove it, and bring God and man together (1 Timothy 2:5; Hebrews 9:26; 1 Peter 3:18). Jesus is now our Advocate in heaven and He ever lives to make intercession for us (1 John 2:1; Hebrews 7:25).

Near the end of the book, Elihu began to speak. Up to that point, he had listened in silence as Job called out for someone to approach God on his behalf. Elihu responded to Job: Although I am a man of clay like you, *"Look, I am the one you were wishing for, someone to stand between you and God and to be both his representative and yours"* (Job 33:6, TLB). Elihu went on to say that when a man suffers with sickness and pain, if he has a mediator, he can be delivered, *"Yet if there is an angel on his side as a mediator, one out of a thousand, to tell a man what is right for him, to be gracious to him and say, 'Spare him from going down to the pit; I have found a ransom for him' then his flesh is renewed like a child's; it is restored as in the days of his youth... he is restored by God to his righteous state...redeemed...from going down to the pit"* (Job 33:23-26,28, NIV). The Amplified Bible says it this way, *"Then [God] is gracious to him, and says, Deliver him from going down into the pit [of destruction]; I have found a ransom [a price of redemption, an atonement]!"* (verse 24). Through his words, Elihu also foreshadowed the person and work of Christ our Redeemer.

The Book of Job recounts the story of a man redeemed from troubles by God as it pictures the coming redemption from sin accomplished through the Cross of Christ. In doing so, Job showcases the goodness of God.

JOB HAD LESS LIGHT

Many of our misconceptions about what happened to Job come from things Job himself said: *"The Lord gave, and the Lord hath taken away; blessed be the name of the Lord"* (Job 1:21). *"Shall we receive good at the hand of God, and shall we not receive evil?"* (Job 2:10). From these and other words Job spoke, many people have concluded that God will give and then take away precious things from His people if He considers it necessary for some higher purpose. Although these statements from Job sound right because we have heard them so often, they are inaccurate.

It is important to understand that although everything in the Bible is truly stated, not everything in the Bible is true. For example, the Pharisees said that Jesus was a sinner: *"They brought to the Pharisees the man who had been blind. Now the day on which Jesus had made the mud and opened the man's eyes was a Sabbath. Therefore the Pharisees also asked him how he had received his sight. 'He put mud on my eyes,' the man replied, 'and I washed, and now I see.' Some of the Pharisees said, 'This man is not from God, for he does not keep the Sabbath.' But others asked, 'How can a sinner do such miraculous signs?...A second time they summoned the man who had been blind. 'Give glory to God,' they said. 'We know this man is a sinner.'"* (John 9:13-16,24, NIV). Was Jesus a sinner? Of course not. Yes, the Pharisees actually made

51

those statements about Jesus, but their remarks were not true. In the same way, Job actually spoke the words recorded in his book, but many of the things he said were not correct. They *cannot* be true statements because they contradict the revelation of God given us in Jesus.

You may wonder: If what Job said was wrong, then why does the Bible say, *"In all of this, Job did not sin or revile God"* (Job 1:22, TLB) and *"In all this did not Job sin with his lips"* (Job 2:10)? These verses do not mean that Job was correct in everything he said. They simply mean that when tragedy struck, Job did not sin by cursing God. "The Lord gives and takes away" is not a sinful statement. It is a declaration based on lack of knowledge.

You might also wonder: Why does the Bible include a book with lots of "misinformation?" "Less information" or "less light" is a better way to put it. Job lived during the time of the Patriarchs (Abraham, Isaac, and Jacob). His picture of God was incomplete. He had no knowledge of Satan working behind the scenes. Job did not know that only good comes from God and that the devil comes to steal, kill, and destroy (James 1:17; John 10:10). Job's story is the first book of the Bible to be recorded. Because God has gradually revealed Himself through the pages of scripture, the Book of Job has less light—important light, but less light—than we have today in Jesus and the New Testament.

Consider this important point in regard to accurately interpreting Job. Although Job's "misinformation" is "less light" to us, for Israel—the people to whom Job was first written—it was "greater light." For the Hebrew people, Job's story was *more* information about God, Satan, and the nature of life in a sin cursed earth. Problems arise for us when we who have the "full light" of God given in Jesus try to interpret our situation through the "lesser light" of Job. We look to Job to try to answer questions the book does not address. We approach Job from the standpoint of, "What does it mean to me? How does it speak to the specific circumstances of my situation? Why did I lose my job? Why was my house damaged by a storm? Why did my loved one die?" Because Job does not address any of those issues, we draw faulty conclusions. Job was written to give Israel hope of deliverance from bondage and to encourage them to remain faithful to God. The first readers of Job would never have asked the kinds of questions about the book that we in the 21st century raise.

Misconceptions about what happened to Job also come from taking his words out of context. Job 23:10 is such a verse. *"But he knoweth the way that I take: when he hath tried me, I shall come forth as gold."* People say this means that God was refining Job with troubles so that he would be purified. But when we read this verse in context, we see that Job was professing his innocence to God. As Job discussed his misfortunes with his friends, he repeatedly said that he had done nothing wrong to merit the kinds of troubles he was experiencing. Job adamantly declared that if God were to examine him, God would see it was so. Chapter 23 begins with Job longing once again to make his case before God: *"If only I knew where to find God, I would go to his throne and talk with him there. I would lay out my case and present my arguments...(but)...I cannot find him...But he knows where I am going. And when he has tested me like gold in a fire, he will pronounce me innocent. For I have stayed in God's paths; I have followed his ways and not turned aside. I have not departed from his commands but have treasured his word in my heart"* (NLT). This is not a man declaring that God is testing him to purify him. This is a man proclaiming his virtues as he explains why he does not deserve what has happened to him. *"But he knows every detail of what is happening to me; and when he has examined me, he will pronounce me completely innocent—as pure as solid gold!"* (verse 10, TLB). *"But he knows where I am and what I've done. He can cross-examine me all he wants, and I'll pass the test with honors"* (verse 10, The Message).

Job 13:15 is another example of a statement made by Job that is misunderstood because it is taken out of context: *"Though he slay me, yet will I trust in him."* People have construed this to mean that God may kill you or allow the devil to kill you for some sovereign reason. But that is not what the verse says. As we mentioned earlier, Job over and over made the point that if he could talk to God, God would realize that he had been unfairly afflicted. When we read the context of the verse we see that because Job did not have a clear view of God, he was concerned that if he spoke boldly to God, God might kill him. Yet, Job was so persuaded of his cause that he was willing to take the risk. *"So hold your tongue while I have my say, then I'll take whatever I have coming to me. Why do I go out on a limb like this and take my life in my hands? Because even if he killed me, I'd keep on hoping. I'd defend my innocence to the very end"* (Job 13:13-15, The Message). *"Yes, I will take my life in my hands and say what I really think. God may kill me for saying this—in fact, I expect him to. Nevertheless, I am going to argue my case with him"* (Job 13:14-15, TLB).

GOD AND THE DEVIL TALK

Besides reading verses out of context, we misinterpret Job because we misunderstand the two conversations between God and the devil recorded at the beginning of the book. From these conversations, people have concluded that God commissioned Satan's attacks on Job. However, that interpretation is contrary to the revelation of God given us in Jesus. There is no hint in the New Testament of Jesus and the devil working together. Quite the opposite is true. Everywhere Jesus went, He *undid* the works of the devil.

The Bible never calls the devil an ally or an instrument of God. The devil is always called an enemy. The name Satan means "adversary." Why would the "archenemy of God and all that is good" (as *Strong's Concordance* refers to Satan) be interested in helping God perfect His people? As we said in Chapter 3, James 4:7 tells us to submit to God and resist the devil. If God sends or allows the devil to afflict, teach, purge, or discipline us, then how can we obey this verse and *resist* the devil yet still receive the teaching, discipline, and purging of God *through* the devil?

Some might ask: "What about 1 Corinthians 5:1-13?" Among the believers at Corinth, there was a man who was sleeping with his father's wife and Paul wrote to tell the church how to deal with the situation. Paul instructed them, *"Shouldn't you be overwhelmed with sorrow? The man who has done such a thing should certainly be expelled from your fellowship! ...the man should be left to the mercy of Satan so that while his body will experience the destructive powers of sin his spirit may yet be saved in the day of the Lord"* (verses 2,5, J.B. Phillips). People argue that God directed Paul to turn the man over to the devil for discipline just as God permitted Satan to work on Job. However, to equate this incident with what happened to Job is an example of not properly interpreting the Word of God.

When Paul said, "Turn the man over to the devil," it was simply another way of saying "put him out of the church." Paul told the Corinthians to expel the man for several reasons. One, so they themselves would not be influenced by his sin (verse 7). Two, because Paul had previously told the Corinthian church not to associate with *"anyone who claims to be a brother Christian but indulges in sexual sins"* (TLB). Three, sin works death in our lives and sowing to the flesh produces corruption in the flesh (Romans 6:23; Galatians 6:7-8). Paul was exhorting the Corinthians: "Put that unrepentant man out from under the protection, fellowship, and blessing of being part of the church. Let him reap the physical consequences of his sin. Hopefully, that will bring him to repentance."

This was a church government issue. It in no way compares to Job's situation. Job had committed no gross sin, he was not excommunicated from anything, and he had no idea why his troubles came on him. The man at Corinth knew exactly what he had done wrong, why he was put out of the church, and why he was reaping negative consequences.

Before we discuss the dialogue between God and the devil, let's read it. The first conversation is found in Job, Chapter 1. *"Now there was a day when the sons of God* (angels) *came to present themselves before the Lord, and Satan came also among them* (v.6). *And the Lord said unto Satan, 'Whence comest thou?' Then Satan answered the Lord, and said, 'From going to and fro in the earth, and from walking up and down in it'* (v.7). *And the Lord said unto Satan, 'Hast thou considered my servant Job, that there is none like him in the earth, a perfect and an upright man, one that feareth God, and eschewed evil'* (v.8)? *Then Satan answered the Lord, and said, 'Doth Job fear God for nought?'* (v.9). *Hast not thou made an hedge about him, and about his house, and about all that he hath on every side? Thou hast blessed the work of his hands, and his substance is increased in the land* (v.10). *But put forth thine hand now, and touch all that he hath, and he will curse thee to thy face"* (v.11).

The second conversation is located in Chapter 2. *"Again there was a day when the sons of God* (angels) *came to present themselves before the Lord, and Satan came also among them to present himself before the Lord* (v.1). *And the Lord said unto Satan, 'From whence comest thou?' And Satan answered the Lord, and said, 'From going to and fro in the earth, and from walking up and down in it'* (v.2). *And the Lord said unto Satan, 'Hast thou considered my servant Job, that there is none like him in the earth, a perfect and an upright man, one that feareth God, and escheweth evil? and still he holdeth fast his integrity, although thou movest me against him, to destroy him without cause'* (v.3). *And Satan answered the Lord, and said, 'Skin for skin, yea, all that a man hath will he give for his life* (v.4). *But put forth thine hand now, and touch his bone and his flesh, and he will curse thee to thy face'* (v.5). *And the Lord said unto Satan, 'Behold, he is in thine hand; but save his life'"* (v.6).

At first glance, these two dialogues are troubling. But whatever these conservations say, they *cannot* mean that God gave the devil permission to do horrible things to His servant Job because that interpretation does not fit with the rest of the Bible and with what Jesus shows us about God. If we take a closer look at each conversation, we will see that God was not responsible for what happened to Job.

The First Conversation

Many say that God initiated Satan's assault by pointing out Job. "*Hast thou considered my servant Job, that there is none like him in the earth, a perfect and an upright man, one that feareth God, and escheweth evil?*" (Job 1:8). Notice, God commended Job's spiritual characteristics but said nothing about his material condition. Yet, Satan knew Job was wealthy (Job 1:9-10). How did Satan know? Because Satan, having just come from wandering the earth, was familiar with Job and was already planning his attack. The word "considered" in Hebrew means "the heart." *"And Jehovah said unto the Adversary, Hast thou set thy heart against my servant Job?"* (Job 1:8, YLT). That agrees with what the New Testament tells us about Satan: *"Be sober, be vigilant; because your adversary the devil, as a roaring lion, walketh about, seeking whom he may devour"* (1 Peter 5:8).

In response to God's commendation of Job's righteous living, Satan scoffed, *"Why shouldn't he* (live right)*, when you pay him so well?"* (Job 1:9, TLB), adding that if all was taken away from Job, he would curse God to His face. God replied, *"Very well, then, everything he has is in your hands, but on the man himself do not lay a finger"* (Job 1:12, NIV). Many believe that God gave the devil permission to assail Job but put a limit on what he could do to Job. That *cannot* be so because it is contrary to the revelation of God given in Jesus. The Lord was simply stating a fact: Job, like all of us, was already in Satan's power because he was born into a fallen race in a sin cursed earth. That interpretation is compatible with what the New Testament says: Adam, through his disobedience in the Garden of Eden, surrendered his God-given authority in the earth to the devil. Jesus referred to Satan as "the prince of this world," and the Apostle Paul called Satan the "god of this world" and "the prince of the power of the air" (Luke 4:6; John 12:31; 2 Corinthians 4:4; Ephesians 2:2).

The Second Conversation

Following the first conversation, Job lost his wealth and his children (Job 1:13-19). Satan went before God a second time and they spoke again. Job 2:3 is a repeat of Job 1:8 with one addition, *"And still he holdeth fast his integrity, although thou movest me against him, to destroy him without cause."* Obviously, Satan has no power to influence God to do anything.

The Septuagint Translation renders this verse: "*Still he retained his innocence; so that thou hast ordered the destruction of his property, without accomplishing thy purpose.*" Despite the calamities that had befallen Job, he remained faithful to God.

"*Then Satan answered the Lord, 'Skin for skin! Yes, all that a man has will he give for his life. But put forth Your hand now, and touch his bone and his flesh, and he will curse and renounce You to Your face.'*" And the Lord said to Satan, 'Behold, he is in your hand; only spare his life'*" (Job 2:4-6, AMP). Some say this verse shows that God has the devil "on a leash" and limits what the devil can do. However, if the devil's tactics don't produce the desired results, God will allow the devil to bring more destruction. In Job's case, God put the limit at: "Just don't kill him!" That *cannot* be the case because Jesus, who is God and shows us God, never did anything like that to anyone.

God was not addressing physical death in this passage. In the Hebrew, the word "life" refers to the inner being with its thoughts and emotions. When applied to a man, it means the whole person. In this passage, God was restating the fact that Job, because he was born in a fallen world, was already in Satan's power. But God was making it clear to the original readers that even though men are in the devil's territory because of Adam's sin, "The devil cannot snatch you from Me or thwart My ultimate plan for you if you will stay faithful to Me."

› →››» · «‹‹‹‹‹ ‹

At first glance, the scene between God and the devil seems to say that God commissioned the devil to afflict Job while restricting what Satan could do to Job. However, as we pointed out in the last chapter, the Holy Spirit inspired Old Testament writers to connect destructive events with God, not because God was the cause of them but to help men see that there is no other god and there is no other power equal to God. Israel lived in a world of idol worshippers. While in Egypt, many Israelites began to worship the Egyptians gods. New information about a powerful Adversary might have caused the Hebrews to think that the devil was another god they could worship. Therefore, these dialogues between God and the devil are portrayed in a way that makes it clear: "I am God Almighty, the only God. Everything, including Satan, is subject to Me. Nothing happens outside of My ultimate control of the universe." That does not mean God causes, commissions, or approves of the evil in this world. It means that nothing takes Him by surprise and nothing happens that He cannot cause to serve His purposes as He gathers His family. To Israel, this was *more* light...reassuring light!

THE END OF JOB

As we pointed out earlier, the only New Testament reference to Job directs us to the end of his story. The idea that God allowed the devil to afflict Job for some sovereign purpose does not fit with the conclusion of the story. At the end of Job's ordeal, God spoke to him from a whirlwind and challenged his ignorance and powerlessness (Job 38:1–40:2; 40:7–41:34). However, the Lord never mentioned Job's afflictions nor did He reveal why evil came on Job. If the standard interpretation of Job is correct, then why is there no mention of Job's suffering in the Lord's words to Job? It's because the Book of Job *is not* about Job's suffering. According to everything else the Bible says in reference to Job, the book is about Job's righteousness, patience, and deliverance at the hand of a loving God (Ezekiel 14:14,20; James 5:11).

Consider the highlights of God's words to Job. God began, *"Why do you confuse the issue? Why do you talk without knowing what you're talking about? Pull yourself together, Job! Up on your feet! Stand tall!"* (Job 38:2-3, The Message). God then asked Job about the marvels of the material creation: "Were you there when I laid the foundations of the earth? Can you explain or control its processes or its creatures?" *"[Since you question the manner of the Almighty's rule] deck yourself now with the excellency and dignity [of the supreme Ruler, and yourself undertake the government of the world if you are so wise], and array yourself with honor and majesty"* (Job 40:10, AMP). *"I'll gladly step aside and hand things over to you—you can surely save yourself with no help from me!"* (Job 40:14, The Message). God rebuked Job for questioning His handling of things. But the "things" God addressed in His speech were not the specific details of Job's situation. Instead God spoke to Job about the wonder of His creation, which expresses His power and wisdom. Why?

Job was a man who, like many of us, was grappling with the randomness and unfairness of life in a sin cursed earth. Although Job lived in obedience to and fear of God, he lost his wealth to lightning strikes and thieves, his children to a violent storm, and his health to a horrific disease. In addition to questions and complaints about his own circumstances, Job saw undeserved suffering all around. *"Why must the godly wait for him in vain? For a crime wave has engulfed us...the donkeys of the poor and fatherless are taken...The needy are kicked aside;...The wicked snatch fatherless children from their mother's breasts... the bones of the dying cry from the city; the wounded cry for help; yet God does not respond to their moaning"* (Job 24:1-13, TLB). Job believed God was mishandling not just *his* life, but life in general.

God's omission of suffering in His rebuke of Job, and His emphasis on His power and wisdom demonstrated through the creation, make sense when we put Job's story in the context of the overall theme of the Bible. God created men to be His sons and He created the earth to be the home for His family. His original plan is off track because of sin. But God is working out His plan to deliver His family and their home from bondage. It may look as though God is mishandling things because specific instances of suffering are not immediately addressed. But the Lord's primary goal at this point in time is not to stop all suffering and make life easy. Rather, it is to bring men and women to saving knowledge of Himself. God's words challenged Job: "Who are you to question the way My plan to redeem mankind and the earth is unfolding? I am God Almighty. I will save you and I will save My family."

The Book of Job doesn't make these exact statements, but verses in other books of the Bible do. When you interpret Job in that *greater* light, it is consistent with what Jesus shows us about God and with the purpose for which Job was originally written—to help Israel. Israel was going to struggle with the same issues as Job when they faced the hardships on the way to the Promised Land after leaving Egypt. Israel was going to question God, complain, and doubt His care of them (Exodus 16:2,7; Numbers 14:1-3). God's first written revelation to Israel was: "It may look like I've mishandled things, but I know what I am doing! I will make things right!"

Job admitted his ignorance and presumption and repented. Notice, however, it was not Job's sufferings that produced a change in him. Job's issues were exposed and changed when God spoke to Him. That's because God corrects and purifies men with *His Word*, not with afflictive circumstances. (We'll discuss that point in more detail later.) Natural things like difficult circumstances don't produce spiritual results. Tragedies don't purify people any more than sitting in church makes people into new creatures.

At the end of Job's ordeal, God revealed Himself to Job as He truly is. In doing so, God gave Job peace of mind that carried him through the final 140 years of his life. *"You ask who it is who has so foolishly denied your providence. It is I. I was talking about things I knew nothing about and did not understand, things far too wonderful for me...I had heard about you before, but now I have seen you...Then at last he died, an old, old man, after living a long, good life"* (Job 42:3,5,17, TLB).

Even with an understanding that God was not behind the tragic circumstances in Job's life, people still may wonder, "If all of these bad things happened to Job—a person described as blameless and upright—will terrible things happen to me?" No one is guaranteed a life that is problem-free. In fact, Jesus said, *"In the world ye shall have tribulation: but be of good cheer; I have overcome the world"* (John 16:33). Despite our troubles and hardships, the Bible promises us that, through Christ, we can stand strong as overcomers in the midst of whatever Satan and life bring our way. God will get us through until He gets us out. Sometimes people try to figure out what Job "did wrong" or how he "let the devil get to him." But the Book of Job was not written to address those issues. Don't be robbed of what Job does say by looking for what it doesn't say.

CONCLUSION

There is much more we could say about the Book of Job, but consider these final thoughts. Job was an awe-inspiring, hope-filled book for the people to whom it was originally written. If we read it in the context of what it meant to Israel and filter it through the greater light of the New Testament, Job will be an awe-inspiring book of hope for us, too. In a sin cursed earth, we—like Job—are going to see and experience things we don't understand. There will be questions about why things happen. But God's words to Job assure us: "Look how big I am. Look at My wisdom. This didn't take Me by surprise. I will work it out. My plan of redemption will be accomplished. Satan cannot foil My plan to have you as sons and to live with you on a perfect earth, fully redeemed from every trace of corruption and death." Job is a "mini picture" of God making things right for Job with the promise that He will ultimately make things right for His family.

It is difficult to read the Book of Job without being influenced by preconceived ideas. But if we can put them aside and read the book in the light of the rest of the Bible, we can get an accurate understanding of Job. And once again, we see that God is good...and good means good.

YES, BUT WHAT ABOUT CHRISTIAN SUFFERING?

At this point, you may be thinking, "Okay, I understand that God didn't send Job's trials. But what about suffering? Isn't suffering for the Lord part of Christian life? Aren't we called to suffer for His Name's sake?" Yes, suffering is part of a Christian's life, but not in the way you may think. The fact is, everyone suffers in this life—Christian or not. Suffering is present in the earth because of Adam and Eve's sin. Their sin had a cataclysmic effect on the human race and on the earth. As a result, there's no such thing as a life without suffering. It's part of life in a sin cursed earth. (See Chapter 3 for a detailed discussion on the effect of sin.)

The New Testament defines suffering for the Lord as being persecuted for our faith in Christ and as any kind of personal sacrifice or discomfort we experience as we live for Him. The Bible speaks of two kinds of suffering in relation to Christians: those things that Jesus suffered for us and those things we suffer for Him. When the New Testament speaks of suffering for the Lord, it never refers to suffering sickness, or a bad marriage, or a car wreck, or a failed business deal. We must always let scripture define scripture. If the Bible doesn't define suffering for the Lord as enduring sickness or difficult relationships, then we have no right to impose these definitions upon the word "suffering."

JESUS SUFFERED FOR US

Jesus Christ suffered certain things for us at the Cross so we don't have to suffer them. Isaiah 53:4-6 says, *"Surely he took up our infirmities and carried our sorrows, yet we considered him stricken by God, smitten by him, and afflicted. But he was pierced for our transgressions, he was crushed for our iniquities; the punishment that brought us peace was upon him, and by his wounds we are healed. We all, like sheep, have gone astray, each of us has turned to his own way; and the Lord has laid on him the iniquity of us all"* (NIV). This passage tells us God laid our iniquities on Jesus at the Cross. The word "iniquity" in the Hebrew is *avon* and it includes not only sin, but the punishment or evil consequences that sin brings. At the Cross, God laid our sin and the consequences of our sin on Jesus.

Galatians 3:13 says, *"Christ hath redeemed us from the curse of the law, being made a curse for us: for it is written, Cursed is every one that hangeth on a tree."* The curse of the Law includes all the consequences of sin listed in Deuteronomy 28— humiliation, barrenness, unfruitfulness, mental and physical sickness, family breakdown, physical and spiritual poverty, opposition, and failure and defeat, among others. Every one of these curses came on Jesus at the Cross so we could be released from them. An exchange took place at the Cross. All the evil due to us because of our sin and disobedience went to Jesus so that all the blessing due to Him for His obedience could come to us. *"He was beaten that we might have peace. He was whipped, and we were healed!"* (Isaiah 53:5, NLT). Many Christians suffer sickness, disease, pain, family breakdown, and defeat and think that in the process, they are suffering for the Lord. But the Bible tells us that Jesus suffered those curses at the Cross so we don't have to bear them.

WE SUFFER FOR HIM

Suffering for the Lord includes the persecution and personal sacrifice we experience as we preach the gospel and live for Jesus Christ. Persecution is part of Christian life. Jesus said, *"Remember the word that I said unto you, The servant is not greater than his lord. If they have persecuted me, they will also persecute you"* (John 15:20). The Apostle Paul wrote, *"Yea, and all that will live godly in Christ Jesus shall suffer persecution"* (2 Timothy 3:12).

Paul also wrote these words in Philippians 1:29: *"For unto you it is given in the behalf of Christ, not only to believe on him, but also to suffer for his sake."* I've heard this verse quoted as proof that Christians must suffer sickness, pain, and tragedies. But based on the very next verse, it's clear that Paul was referring to suffering persecution.

He goes on to say, *"Having the same conflict which ye saw in me, and now hear to be in me."* In Philippians 1:30, Paul states that the Philippians were fighting the same battle they had seen him fight and heard he was now fighting. When Paul wrote these words he was in prison in Rome for proclaiming the good news of the resurrection of Jesus Christ. At that time, he didn't know if he'd be released or executed. Notice, Paul refers not just to the conflict the Philippians had *heard* about, but to the conflict they *saw* in him. What had they seen? Several years earlier, Paul visited the city of Philippi and was thrown in jail for casting a devil out of a servant girl (Acts 16:12-34). The Philippians had seen Paul jailed for preaching the gospel and now they heard he was in a Roman prison for his preaching. That is what Paul meant by "suffering for the Lord's sake."

In Romans 8:17, Paul speaks of suffering *with* Christ: *"If we are his children then we are God's heirs, and all that Christ inherits will belong to all of us as well! Yes, if we share in his sufferings we shall certainly share in his glory"* (J.B. Phillips). The only suffering we can share with Jesus is persecution. When Jesus appeared to Saul (who became Paul) on the road to Damascus, Saul was on his way to arrest Christians. Jesus told Saul that persecuting Christians was the same as persecuting Him. *"But on his journey, as he neared Damascus, a light from the sky suddenly blazed around him, and he fell to the ground. Then he heard a voice speaking to him, 'Saul, Saul, why are you persecuting me?' 'Who are you Lord?' he asked. 'I am Jesus whom you are persecuting,' was the reply"* (Acts 9:4-5, J.B. Phillips). Christians are the Body of Christ and we're joined to the Head, the Lord Jesus Christ. When the Body is persecuted, so is the Head.

In the Book of Acts, we see that the first followers of Jesus experienced two types of suffering. They suffered beatings, jail, slander, and death for preaching the gospel. They also suffered physical discomforts due to the hardships of travel, obstacles they faced, and possessions they sacrificed as they took the news of Jesus' death, burial, and resurrection to the world. We see this in Acts 5 when the Jewish leadership in Jerusalem arrested the apostles for performing miracles in the name of Jesus. That night, an angel set the apostles free and told them to go into the Temple and proclaim the message of Jesus. When the religious authorities heard that the apostles were preaching in the Temple, they captured them and brought the apostles before the council. *"And when they had called the apostles, and beaten them, they commanded that they should not speak in the name of Jesus, and let them go. And they departed from the presence of the council, rejoicing that they were counted worthy to suffer shame for his name"* (Acts 5:40-41). Suffering for the Lord is clearly defined in this incident as persecution for preaching the gospel. (See Note 5 for more details on suffering for the Lord.)

⸱ →꯭꯭꯭꯭↠ ⸱ ↞꯭꯭꯭꯭꯭ ⸱

There are no examples in the Book of Acts of the first Christians referring to sickness, physical infirmity, relational issues, or other such hardships as "suffering for the Lord." When the apostles spoke and wrote about suffering for the Lord in Acts and the epistles, their context was suffering persecution and hardships connected with preaching the gospel—the same kinds of sufferings they had experienced.

A CHOSEN VESSEL

People sometimes say the Apostle Paul was a chosen vessel picked by the Lord for special suffering and that Christians may be chosen for such suffering too. But the Bible doesn't support this belief. Scripture says Paul was a chosen vessel called to preach the gospel. *"But the Lord said unto him, Go thy way: for he is a chosen vessel unto me, to **bear my name** before the Gentiles, and kings, and the children of Israel: For I will show him how great things he must suffer for my name's sake"* (Acts 9:15-16). From Paul's conversion in Acts 9 to the end of the Book of Acts, we get a detailed account of the things Paul suffered. The sufferings Paul went through consisted of persecution and the difficulties connected with preaching and spreading the gospel. Paul had to experience those things—not to be perfected or chastened or humbled—but to bring salvation, healing, and deliverance to people.

Paul acknowledged why he experienced so much suffering in his life. *"But if we are afflicted, it is for your comfort and salvation"* (2 Corinthians 1:6, NASB). He went on to refer to persecutions he endured in Asia (specifically at the city of Ephesus in Acts 19:21-41): *"For we do not want you to be uninformed, brethren, about the affliction and oppressing distress which befell us in [the province of] Asia, how we were so utterly and unbearably weighed down and crushed that we despaired even of life [itself]"* (2 Corinthians 1:8, AMP).

Shortly before he was martyred, Paul wrote a letter from prison to Timothy, his son in the faith. He told Timothy, *"This is my gospel, for which I am suffering even to the point of being chained like a criminal. But God's word is not chained. Therefore I endure everything for the sake of the elect, that they too may obtain the salvation that is in Christ Jesus, with eternal glory"* (2 Timothy 2:8-10, NIV). Paul was suffering because he preached the gospel, but he was willing to endure the hardships so that people could hear about salvation through Jesus Christ.

The suffering Paul experienced in his lifetime was not an end in itself but rather a means to an end. Paul didn't suffer for a sovereign purpose known only to God. He suffered as he preached the good news of salvation to as many people as possible. Because of the call on some people's lives, they may, like Paul, have to go through extraordinary circumstances to preach the gospel. But that suffering is not orchestrated by God.

Paul also wrote to the Colossians: *"[Even] now I rejoice in the midst of my sufferings on your behalf. And in my own person I am making up whatever is still lacking and remains to be completed [on our part] of Christ's afflictions, for the sake of His body, which is the church"* (Colossians 1:24, AMP). Notice these key points about Paul's statement. Paul said he suffered for the Colossians. What did he suffer for them? Persecution and the difficulties he faced as he proclaimed the message of Jesus. Paul said he suffered what remained to be suffered of Christ's afflictions. Jesus' sufferings on the Cross—when He took our sins, sicknesses, and punishment on Himself—were His alone to bear and they were completed when He rose from the dead. The only sufferings of Christ that Paul or any of us can participate in are persecution and hardships as we preach the gospel. Remember, Jesus said that He considers the persecution of Christians the same as persecuting Him because we are His Body.

PAUL'S THORN IN THE FLESH

Our discussion of Paul's sufferings leads us to one of the most debated topics in the Bible, Paul's thorn in the flesh: *"And lest I should be exalted above measure through the abundance of the revelations, there was given to me a thorn in the flesh, the messenger of Satan to buffet me, lest I should be exalted above measure"* (2 Corinthians 12:7). Many people believe that Paul's thorn in the flesh was a disease sent by God to keep Paul humble. But the verse clearly explains that Paul's thorn in the flesh was the messenger of Satan. Messenger, in the Greek (the original language of the New Testament), is the word *aggelos*.

Aggelos appears 188 times in scripture and it always means a "being" or a "personality." It never means a "disease." The word "thorn" is used in the Old Testament and New Testament literally and figuratively. In some cases, the word refers to an actual thorn. In other cases, the word refers to troublesome people (Numbers 33:55; Joshua 23:13; Judges 2:3). Paul said

71

that this "messenger" or "angel" came from Satan, not God. From the context, we can see that the thorn was a troublesome being from Satan sent to harass Paul.

Paul tells us that he asked the Lord three times to take the thorn away. The Lord's answer was, *"My grace is sufficient for thee: for my strength is made perfect in weakness,"* to which Paul responded, *"Most gladly therefore will I rather glory in my infirmities, that the power of Christ may rest upon me"* (2 Corinthians 12:9). Paul referred to the opposition from the messenger as an infirmity. What exactly is an infirmity? Some say it was an eye disease that God refused to heal. But we can't forget one of our key principles for reading the Bible: We must let scripture define scripture.

Just a few verses before the "thorn in the flesh" reference, Paul offered a detailed list of the infirmities he suffered: *"Are they ministers of Christ? (I speak as a fool) I am more; in labours more abundant, in stripes above measure, in prisons more frequent, in deaths oft. Of the Jews five times received I forty stripes save one. Thrice was I beaten with rods, once was I stoned, thrice I suffered shipwreck, a night and a day I have been in the deep; In journeyings often, in perils of waters, in perils of robbers, in perils by mine own countrymen, in perils by the heathen, in perils in the city, in perils in the wilderness, in perils in the sea, in perils among false brethren; In weariness and painfulness, in watchings often, in hunger and thirst, in fastings often, in cold and nakedness. Besides those things that are without, that which cometh upon me daily, the care of all the churches. Who is weak, and I am not weak? who is offended, and I burn not? If I must needs glory, I will glory of the things which concern my infirmities"* (2 Corinthians 11:23-30). Notice, he does not list sickness and disease as one of his infirmities.

Those who believe that Paul's thorn was an eye disease often refer to Galatians 4:15, which says: *"Where is then the blessedness ye spake of? for I bear you record, that, if it had been possible, ye would have plucked out your own eyes, and have given them to me."* They say Paul made this statement because of the willingness of the Galatian people to go so far as to give him their own eyes in order to save Paul from his serious eye condition.

Galatia was a province in Asia Minor. In the Galatian city of Lystra, Paul was stoned for preaching the gospel and left for dead. Despite this severe stoning, Paul got up, went with his fellow minister, Barnabas, and the next day walked about 15 miles to the city of Derbe. He then went back and preached at Lystra and two other cities (Acts 14:19-21). When Paul preached to the people in these cities, he had just undergone a horrific stoning and although he was raised up, he still had physical evidence of the bruises and cuts from his ordeal. Paul himself said, *"From now on let no person trouble me...for I bear on my body the [brand] marks of the Lord Jesus [the wounds, scars, and other outward evidence of persecutions— these testify to His ownership of me]!"* (Galatians 6:17, AMP). The eye troubles Paul experienced were the result of his recent stoning, not an eye disease.

By now you might be thinking, "Well, whatever the thorn was, God gave it to Paul keep him humble." There are some problems with that idea. One, the Bible says the thorn came from Satan, not God. Secondly, 2 Corinthians 12:7 says the thorn was given to Paul to keep him from *being* exalted, not to keep him from *exalting himself.* Let's explore this thought a bit further. Paul had received tremendous revelation from God (2 Corinthians 12:1-4). Satan did not want Paul's revelation to be accepted when Paul proclaimed his message, so he sent an angelic being (a fallen angel, a devil) to harass Paul. That is consistent with the description of events in the Book of Acts. Paul would go to a city to preach, someone or something would stir up the crowd, and Paul would be mobbed, put in jail, or thrown out of town (Acts 13:45; 14:2-6; 19:21-41).

Satan always comes to steal the Word of God in and through the difficulties of life. (We discussed how Satan works in Chapter 3.) Paul said that the thorn came from Satan *"lest I be exalted above measure."* The word "exalted" in the Greek is made up of two words, *huper* which means "above" and *airo* which means "to lift." Knowledge from God's Word can lift anyone, including Paul, above the hardships and challenges of life. Satan came to steal the Word of God from Paul through the thorn in the flesh in an attempt to keep Paul from being lifted up above—from being victorious in the midst of extremely harsh circumstances. But Satan's efforts against Paul were unfruitful. Paul called the many difficulties he faced as he preached the gospel "momentary and light." They did not weigh him down. He said that he didn't look at what he *could* see, but at what he *could not* see (2 Corinthians 4:17-18). By focusing on the Word of God, which reveals God's unseen power and provision, Paul was lifted up above the numerous trials he faced in his life. Paul's own testimony was: "God's grace is sufficient for me. His strength is made perfect in my weakness" (2 Corinthians 12:9).

I've had people ask, "Why didn't God just remove Paul's thorn in the flesh when Paul asked for it to be removed—especially if it was a messenger from Satan meant to keep Paul down?" When Paul asked God to remove the thorn, he was asking God to do something God has not promised. God hasn't promised to take the devil away at this point in time. The Bible says that the devil is the god of this world and will continue his activities up to the time that Jesus returns to this earth. Until then, God tells us that our defense is to resist the devil. *"Submit yourselves therefore to God. Resist the devil, and he will flee from you"* (James 4:7). God tells us that His grace toward us and for us is sufficient to deal with anything the devil brings our way.

PERFECTED AND PURGED THROUGH SUFFERING?

The idea of Christian suffering is often misunderstood because people believe we have to endure hardships in order for God to teach, perfect, and purge us. Christians sometimes cite Israel and their wilderness experience as an example of suffering designed by the Lord to help His people grow and mature. But as we study their story, we find that the Israelites refused to enter the Promised Land and had to wander in the wilderness 40 years because of their rebellion and unbelief (Numbers 14:22-35). Their wilderness journey was not a result of God leading them there for a special purpose. In fact, the Bible doesn't commend Israel for their wilderness experience. Instead, we're warned not to follow their example or to duplicate their experience (Hebrews 3:17-19; 4:1-2,11).

God teaches us and perfects us by His Spirit through His Word, not by sending or allowing afflictions. The Holy Spirit is the Teacher of the Church (John 14:26) and His teaching tool is the Word of God (Ephesians 6:17). *"All scripture is given by inspiration of God, and is profitable for **doctrine**, for **reproof**, for **correction**, for **instruction** in righteousness: That the man of God may be perfect, thoroughly furnished unto all good works"* (2 Timothy 3:16-17). God has given ministry gifts to the church—apostles, prophets, evangelists, pastors, and teachers—*"for the **perfecting** of the saints"* (Ephesians

75

4:11-12). As the ministry gifts administer the Word of God by preaching and teaching, the Holy Spirit, through the Word, perfects or matures the saints.

God purifies us with His Word. *"Husbands, love your wives, even as Christ also loved the church, and gave himself for it; That he might sanctify and* **cleanse it with the washing of water by the word***, That he might present it to himself a glorious church, not having spot, or wrinkle, or any such thing; but that it should be holy and without blemish"* (Ephesians 5:25-27). Jesus told his disciples, *"Now are ye* **clean through the word** *which I have spoken unto you"* (John 15:3). Notice what verse 2 says. *"Every branch in me that beareth not fruit he taketh away: and every branch that beareth fruit, he purgeth it, that it may bring forth more fruit."* Some Christians believe that God purges us through suffering so that we can be more productive for Him. But Jesus says in verse 3 that His followers are cleansed by His Word. The words "purge" and "clean" are the same Greek word. Jesus cleanses us or purges us with His Word.

Hebrews 5:8 is sometimes referenced to support the idea that Jesus learned obedience through suffering and, therefore, we should expect to learn through suffering. *"Though he were a Son, yet learned he obedience by the things which he suffered."* This verse can't mean that Jesus was disobedient to the Father and had to suffer in order to learn to obey. The Bible says that Jesus was perfectly obedient to the Father in everything (John 8:29). So, what does the scripture mean? Hebrew 5:7 provides more context. *"During the days of Jesus' life on earth, he offered up prayers and petitions with loud cries and tears to the one who could save him from death, and he was heard because of his reverent submission"* (NIV). This verse refers to Jesus' experience in the Garden of Gethsemane where He prayed with great passion to His Father, *"O my Father, if it be possible, let this cup pass from me: nevertheless, not as I will, but as thou wilt"* (Matthew 26:39).

The Bible says that Jesus, in His humanity, was tempted in all points as we are but was without sin. As the hour of His crucifixion came closer, and aware of the horrors that lay ahead, Jesus was faced with the temptation to abandon God's will for His life and refuse to go to the Cross. Yet, He defeated the temptation by submitting to the Father's will. It's in this context that the Bible says Jesus learned obedience through what He suffered. Jesus experienced what it's like—as a man— to obey God at great cost, even to the point of great suffering to Himself. Other translations of Hebrews 5:8 emphasize this point: *"Son though he was, he had to prove the meaning of obedience through all that he suffered"* (J.B. Phillips). The New Testament in Basic English says *"Through the pain which he underwent, the knowledge came to him of what it was to be under God's orders."*

Jesus' life is an example to us of how we are to view and handle suffering. Just as Jesus obeyed His Father at great cost, so we are to obey our heavenly Father—even if it means we must sacrifice our own desires to remain obedient. When Jesus suffered at the hands of His persecutors, He responded to them in love and committed Himself to His Father: *"To this you were called, because Christ suffered for you, leaving you an example, that you should follow in his steps. 'He committed no sin, and no deceit was found in his mouth.' When they hurled their insults at him, he did not retaliate; when he suffered, he made no threats. Instead, he entrusted himself to him who judges justly"* (1 Peter 2:21-23, NIV). When we suffer persecution, we are to respond like Jesus did by relying on the help of the Holy Spirit.

Perhaps you've heard people say that when we suffer sickness and pain, bad marriages, lack, and other negative circumstances in life, these are just the "crosses we have to bear." But there's no need for mankind to bear the cross of sickness, pain, and many of the other effects of life in an earth damaged by sin. Jesus bore sickness and pain and all the curse of sin on His Cross so we don't have to bear it.

The Bible does say that we are to take up our cross: *"If any man will come after me, let him deny himself, and take up his cross daily, and follow me"* (Luke 9:23). But what is the cross we're told to take up? For Jesus, His Cross was, among other things, the place of complete submission to the will of the Father. Similarly, your cross is the place of complete submission and obedience to the will of God for your life. When Jesus said "Daily take up your cross," He was not referring to sickness, pain, and suffering. Jesus was telling His disciples, "If you want to follow Me, you must deny your will and your way and daily choose the place of total submission to the will of the Father in every area of your life."

WE WILL SUFFER

Why then do sincere, obedient, committed Christians often find themselves in difficult places? There are many answers to that question, but consider these thoughts. It goes without saying that life in a sin cursed earth is hard. That means there is no easy way for any of us to get where we are going in this life—not because God is sending or purposefully allowing suffering, but because we live in a world that has been radically affected by sin. The road can be rough because there is only one way to get to your destination and that way will include life's unexpected hardships. The only way for Israel to get from Egypt to the Promised Land was by crossing the Sinai Peninsula, a dry, mountainous region. Israel had to deal with all the challenges presented by such a landscape. The road can be rough because of persecution. Shadrach, Meshach, and Abednigo were thrown into a fiery furnace by a wicked king, not because God was trying to purify them in the fire but because they refused to worship a false god. The way can be rough because there are those in the wilderness who need our assistance and we have to go in and help them. Paul went many places that brought him great suffering, but he did it to bring people out of darkness into the light of Christ.

The way can also be rough because of our own poor choices. Israel was in the wilderness because of bad choices, unbelief, and disobedience. If you are in a wilderness journey because of unbelief and disobedience, make it a priority to repent and get out. Years of bad choices are usually not undone overnight by making one good choice. It will take time and a series of good choices to change your circumstances, but it will be worth it. Remember this as you walk out of your wilderness: Israel's poor choices brought them to the wilderness. Yet, despite their decisions, God still showed Israel His goodness. He cared for them as a Father and continually met their needs. *"In the desert...you saw how the Lord your God carried you, as a father carries his son, all the way you went until you reached this place. The Lord your God has blessed you in all the works of your hands. He has watched over your journey through this vast desert. These forty years the Lord your God has been with you, and you have not lacked anything"* (Deuteronomy 1:31; 2:7, NIV).

So yes, we do suffer for Christ. The New Testament is clear about this fact. However, the sufferings Christians face are the persecutions and personal sacrifices that come as a result of choosing to live for the Lord. The negative circumstances of life—such as sickness, difficult relationships, pain, loss, and other hardships—are part of life in an earth filled with sin and are challenges that affect all people. Hardships and troubles are part of life in a sin cursed earth, but none of this suffering comes from the hand of God.

When we do experience suffering as we live for Christ and preach the gospel, the Bible promises that God will provide power, strength, and deliverance in those times. The Apostle Paul captures the promise of God's help and protection—in all circumstances—in his words to the Christians in Rome: *"Who shall separate us from the love of Christ? shall tribulation, or distress, or persecution, or famine, or nakedness, or peril, or sword? As it is written, For thy sake we are killed all the day long; we are accounted as sheep for the slaughter. Nay, in all these things **we are more than conquerors through him that loved us**"* (Romans 8:35-37). Paul also wrote, *"But thou hast fully known my doctrine, manner of life, purpose, faith, longsuffering, charity, patience, persecutions, afflictions, which came unto me at Antioch, at Iconium, at Lystra; what persecutions I endured: **but out of them all the Lord delivered me**"* (2 Timothy 3:10-11).

YES, BUT WHAT ABOUT CHASTENING?

"Okay, maybe God doesn't give us crosses to bear or make us suffer in order to perfect us, but what about His correction and discipline? Doesn't He sometimes send troubles our way to punish us for wrongdoing so we won't keep making the same mistakes?" How do we answer these questions?

Yes, the Bible does say that God corrects and disciplines His children. The term used in the scriptures is "chasten," a word and concept that is often misunderstood. Many people believe the Lord's chastening involves the use of afflictive circumstances—such as car accidents and cancer—to bring discipline and correction into our lives. People believe and express sentiments like: "I had a car accident. The Lord must be chastening me." Or, "My loved one has cancer. The Lord must be chastening him." But this isn't what chastening means in the New Testament.

The Greek word translated "chastening" in the New Testament is *paideia*. The bold words in the following verses indicate where the word *paideia* was used in the original language. In

Egyptians, and was mighty in words and in deeds." In Ephesians 6:4, "*And, ye fathers, provoke not your children to wrath: but bring them up in the **nurture** and admonition of the Lord.*" In 2 Timothy 3:16, "*All scripture is given by inspiration of God, and is profitable for doctrine, for reproof, for correction, for **instruction** in righteousness.*" In Titus 2:12, "***Teaching** us that, denying ungodliness and worldly lusts, we should live soberly, righteously, and godly, in this present world.*" From these scriptures, it's clear that chastening means instruction, learning, nurturing, and teaching—not accidents, sickness, and tragedy. God doesn't discipline us by sending difficult circumstances our way. God disciplines and chastens us with His Word.

Remember that Jesus *is* God and *shows* us God. Jesus was and is the will of God in action, so we can look at His life to see how God disciplines people. When we look at Jesus' earth ministry, we don't find a single example of Jesus chastening people by making them sick or by allowing disasters into their lives to teach them lessons. When Jesus was on earth and got upset with someone's behavior, He told them about it immediately. Jesus chastened, disciplined, and corrected people with His Words. If that is how Jesus chastened and disciplined people—and Jesus' actions reflect those of our Heavenly Father—then we know this must also be the way the Father disciplines and chastens individuals. Jesus said He only did what He saw His Father do.

About 60 years after Jesus left this earth, He appeared in a vision to His disciple John who was exiled on the Isle of Patmos. The information John received from Jesus at that time became the Book of Revelation. In Revelation, Jesus gave John specific instructions for seven churches that were located in Asia Minor. These instructions, or "letters" as they are often called, contained Jesus' praise and correction for the seven churches. Read the letters and you'll see that Jesus' correction of these churches and their members came through His Words to them.

Jesus concluded His messages to the seven churches with this statement: *"As many as I love, I rebuke and chasten: be zealous therefore, and repent"* (Revelation 3:19). Rebuke and chastening are verbal instructions. To rebuke means to reprove, to scold, or to express disapproval of. To chasten means to train, to instruct, or to correct or discipline by instruction. When Jesus made this statement, He had just finished rebuking and chastening the churches to whom these messages were addressed. He rebuked and chastened them with His Words. The Father also rebukes us and chastens us with His Word. David said in Psalm 39:11, *"When thou with **rebukes** doest correct a man for iniquity."* Psalm 94:12 says, *"Blessed is the man whom thou **chastenest**, O Lord, and **teachest** him out of thy law."*

When Jesus said, *"As many as I love, I rebuke and chasten,"* He linked rebuke and chastening because they are two sides of the same coin. The purpose of rebuke and chastening is to identify and expose unacceptable behaviors so they can be corrected. God's chastening has nothing to do with bad circumstances. Chastisement is discipline for the purpose of instruction, provided through words. Words must be involved so instruction can occur.

Think about it in your everyday life. What if you had a child who misbehaved and you slapped him in the face but didn't tell him what he had done to cause you to hit him? Would he learn anything? Would that be effective parenting? Of course not. Yet, many people accuse God of acting like a parent who punishes His children for no clear reason. Trouble strikes and they assume the Lord is chastening them. They're often not sure what they've done or how to change whatever needs to change, but they're certain the Lord is disciplining them for a sovereign reason known only to Him. When good earthly parents chasten or discipline their children, they tell them what they did wrong and how to correct the problem. In other words, they train and instruct them. That is how God, our Father, treats us.

DOES GOD SPANK US?

Some have said, "Yes, but there are times when God has to spank us just as a human parent spanks a disobedient child." People who hold this belief often quote Hebrews 12:5-7, "*And ye have forgotten the exhortation which speaketh unto you as unto children, My son, despise not thou the chastening of the Lord, nor faint when thou art rebuked of him: For whom the Lord loveth he chasteneth, and scourgeth every son whom he receiveth. If ye endure chastening, God dealeth with you as with sons; for what son is he whom the father chasteneth not?*" There is a huge difference between being spanked on the bottom as a child and getting cancer or having your house burn down. No earthly father in his right mind would "spank" his kid with cancer or a car wreck to teach him a lesson. Jesus told us our Heavenly Father is better than the best earthly father.

As with every verse in the Bible, we must read this passage about chastening in context. It is part of the Epistle to the Hebrews, a letter written to Jewish Christians who were experiencing persecution for their faith and had grown weary under the pressure. Some of them had gone back to Judaism and had rejected Christ and His sacrifice. Others were considering doing the same. This letter was written to offer correction and instruction and to encourage the readers to remain faithful to Jesus. A number of times the author says: "Listen to what God is telling you. Don't fall away." At the end of the letter the author writes, "*Brothers, I urge you to bear with my word of*

84

exhortation, for I have written you only a short letter" (Hebrews 13:22, NIV). To exhort means to admonish, to advise of a fault, or to reprove. All of these actions are done with words, not accidents and tragedies. In other words, the writer urges his readers to accept the discipline, correction, and instruction (or chastening) given in the letter.

Let's look at some key points in Hebrews 12:5-7. Verse 5 says the readers and hearers of the letter are not to despise the chastening of the Lord. Remember, the word "chasten" is *paideia*, the same word translated as "instruction" elsewhere in the New Testament. If we read all of verse 5, we see that the verse itself defines chastening as rebuke: *"My son, despise not thou the chastening of the Lord, nor faint when thou art rebuked of him."* A rebuke is verbal and is accomplished with words. *Despise* means "to have little regard for" in the original Greek: *"My son, do not regard lightly the discipline of the Lord"* (NASB). You can lightly regard words of correction and instruction, but how can you disregard a car wreck or cancer?

Verse 6 says the Lord chastens and scourges his sons. The word "scourge" means to "flog" or "whip" and is used literally and figuratively in the New Testament. In this passage, the word is used figuratively. God scourges us, flogs us, or whips us with His Word. Consider this statement in Jeremiah 23:29, *"Is not my word like as a fire? saith the Lord; and like a hammer that breaketh the rock in pieces?"* Most of us have been "hit" or "flogged" with God's Word at some point in our lives. Have you ever heard a verse during a sermon that made you see an area of your life that needed to change? When that happens, the preacher's words can make us feel like the wind has been knocked out of us. This is an example of being scourged by the Lord through His Word.

In verse 7, the author encourages the readers to endure chastening. To "endure" literally means "to stay under" or "to persevere." Remember, the author wrote this letter to exhort the Jewish Christians to stay faithful to the Lord despite the persecution they were experiencing. The people who received this letter had a choice to accept or reject the discipline of the Lord contained in the letter. Since the Lord's chastening comes through His Word, we can all choose to reject it. We can't "reject" a car wreck or cancer.

In Hebrews 12:8-9, we find a clear definition of the word "chasten." *"For if you had no experience of the correction which all sons have to bear you might well doubt the legitimacy of your sonship. After all, when we were children we had fathers who corrected us, and we respected them for it. Can we not much more readily submit to the discipline of the Father of men's souls, and learn how to live?"* (J.B. Phillips). This passage defines chastisement as correction, the kind of correction that fathers give their sons. Verse 9 puts clear parameters on God's discipline by comparing it to discipline done by human fathers. What earthly father would discipline his child with sickness or tragedies? What earthly father would put his child through years of suffering without the child ever knowing why the hardships are happening? If human parents know how to treat their children properly, how much more does God the Father know how to treat His children? If you wouldn't use troubles and tragedies to discipline your child, then neither will God.

DISOBEDIENCE HAS CONSEQUENCES

In all of this, I'm not saying that there are no physical consequences to sin and disobedience. Romans 6:23 says the wages of sin is death. When you sin, death works in your life. The Bible is very clear that if we sow to the flesh we will reap corruption (Galatians 6:8). If we do not respond to the discipline of the Lord, correct our behavior, and obey His Word, we will reap the consequences of our disobedience.

We see an example of this in 1 Corinthians 11:30-32, the only place in the New Testament where sickness is mentioned in connection with chastening: *"For this cause many are weak and sickly among you, and many sleep. For if we would judge ourselves, we should not be judged. But when we are judged, we are chastened of the Lord, that we should not be condemned with the world."* If we study the whole passage we see that Paul was rebuking the church at Corinth for the way people were conducting communion. The Corinthians were not acknowledging the true purpose of communion. It was supposed to be a remembrance *"representing and signifying and proclaiming the fact of the Lord's death until He comes [again]"* (1 Corinthians 11:26, AMP). But the Corinthians were engaging in strife, drunkenness, and gluttony during this holy assembly.

Paul reprimanded the Corinthians for their communion services because of their irreverence. In verse 27 he said: *"Wherefore whosoever shall eat this bread, and drink this cup of the Lord, unworthily, shall be guilty of the body and blood of the Lord."* In the Greek language, "unworthily" means "irreverently." Their irreverence and failure to recognize the significance of Jesus' sacrifice on the Cross brought judgment in the form of sickness and death: *"Anyone who eats and drinks without discriminating and recognizing with due appreciation that [it is Christ's] body, eats and drinks a sentence (a verdict of judgment) upon himself"* (1 Corinthians 11:29, AMP).

Did God make the Corinthians sick to chasten them? No. God does not make anyone sick. Jesus clearly shows us this.

The Corinthians, through their irreverence, despised the source of healing and life, the Cross of Christ. As a result, they experienced the consequences of not recognizing and acknowledging the value of Christ's sacrifice. This sickness and death was totally preventable. According to the scripture, the Corinthians could have judged themselves and repented and avoided the sickness and death they were experiencing: *"For if we would judge ourselves, we should not be judged"* (1 Corinthians 11:31).

Men truly have free will. Consequences come with every choice. God did not intervene when the choice produced negative outcomes. He allowed them to reap the fruit of their sin so they wouldn't be condemned with the world. This emphasizes the seriousness of their sin. By their actions they were disdaining the Lord's death, their only source of salvation. God let them experience the consequence of their sin in the hope of bringing them to repentance. This is a very different picture than the idea of God chastening us by orchestrating disease and bad circumstances in our lives for a sovereign purpose known only to Him.

God disciplines and chastens us with His Word to correct and instruct us. If God is disciplining you, you will know exactly what the problem is and how to correct it—through His Word. It's important that we have an accurate view of how God chastens us so we can face life with the confidence that God is good...and good means good.

YES, BUT WHAT ABOUT GOD'S TESTS?

*P*eople sometimes talk to me about the trials they believe God has sent into their lives to test and strengthen their faith and to make them patient. However, tests and trials do not come from God. Let me remind you of what we discussed in Chapter 3. Tests and trials are part of life in an earth that has been adversely affected by sin. They are ultimately traceable back to Satan as the first rebel in the universe. Remember also that Satan works through trials, tribulation, affliction, and persecution to try to steal the Word of God from us. If you are unclear about any of this information, you might want to reread Chapter 3 before you continue with this chapter. God does test us, strengthen us, and give us patience. But He does it through His Word and by His Spirit in us.

STRENGTHENED THROUGH TRIALS?

Some say that the storms of life are sent to strengthen us. In Matthew 7:24-27, Jesus spoke of two houses that were battered by a severe storm. One house was destroyed by the storm and the other house survived. The same storm had a very different effect on each house. If storms are meant to strengthen us, then why was one house destroyed? The storms of life in and of themselves do not bring good to us. Life's challenges can and often do destroy many people, including Christians.

According to Jesus, the house that survived the storm was built on a rock and the house that fell was built on sand. Jesus compared the person who hears the Word of God but does not obey to the house built on sand. This person will not be able to withstand the storms of life. On the other hand, a person who hears and obeys the Word of God is like a house built on a rock, fully able to endure a storm.

God does not send storms (destructive circumstances) into our lives as a way to strengthen us. The power to withstand the tribulations and trials of life comes from hearing and doing the Word of God. Proverbs 24:3 says, *"Through wisdom is an house builded; and by understanding it is established."* Wisdom and understanding to deal with the storms of life come from the Word of God. Strength to overcome in the hard times comes from the Word of God. *"I write to you, young men, because you are strong, and the word of God lives in you, and you have overcome the evil one"* (1 John 2:14, NIV).

On one of his missionary journeys, Paul went to the city of Thessalonica and preached the gospel. Many people were converted to Christ. However, after just a few weeks, severe persecution broke out and Paul was forced to leave the city. Paul was concerned for the well-being of his converts, so he sent his fellow minister, Timothy, back to the city to check on the new Christians. *"And we sent Timothy, our brother and God's servant in [spreading] the good news (the Gospel) of Christ, to strengthen and establish and to exhort and comfort and encourage you in your faith, That no one [of you] should be disturbed and beguiled and led astray by these afflictions and difficulties [to which I have referred]"* (1 Thessalonians 3:2-3, AMP). Paul sent Timothy to share the Word of God with the Thessalonians because he knew that it is God's Word that strengthens people in the midst of their difficulties and trials.

Paul recognized that the persecutions the Thessalonians were experiencing had the potential to destroy them if they did not respond properly. He did not say: "Hang on fellows! These trials are going to strengthen you." Paul was aware that Satan was behind their afflictions and was trying to steal the Word of God from them. *"For this reason, when I could stand it no longer, I sent to find out about your faith. I was afraid that in some way the tempter* (Satan) *might have tempted you and our efforts might have been useless"* (1 Thessalonians 3:5, NIV).

Paul understood that it isn't outward circumstances that strengthen us, but rather the inward working of God by His Spirit through His Word. On another occasion, Paul prayed for the Christians at Ephesus that God *"Out of his glorious riches...strengthen you with power through his Spirit in your inner being"* (Ephesians 3:16, NIV). Paul also prayed for the Colossian church, *"That you will be strengthened with his glorious power so that you will have all the patience and endurance you need"* (Colossians 1:11, NLT). If trials bring strength, Paul would have asked God to give these people afflictions to strengthen them. Instead, he prayed for God to strengthen them by His Spirit *in* them.

God does not send trials to strengthen us. He expects us to be strengthened inwardly by His Word, His Spirit, and His power so we can come through the trials of life victoriously.

THE TESTING OF OUR FAITH

Some might ask, "What about the testing of our faith? If we don't have trials, then how does God test our confidence in Him?" Always remember that God's test is His Word. Jesus—who is God and who demonstrates God's will—shows us that. When Jesus was on this earth, He tested His followers with His Word.

In John 6:5-14, a multitude of people had followed Jesus and there was no food for them to eat. Prior to multiplying fish and loaves to feed the crowd, Jesus asked His disciple Philip, *"'Where shall we buy bread for these people to eat?' He asked this only to test him, for he already had in mind what he was going to do"* (verses 5-6, NIV). Jesus asked this question of Philip to give him and the other disciples an opportunity to express confidence in God that He would meet their need in this situation. Jesus tested Philip with His Word.

By this point in His ministry, Jesus had already taught extensively about a Heavenly Father who loves and cares for His people and will meet the material needs of those who seek first the kingdom of God and His righteousness (Matthew 6:25-33). Jesus' test to His disciples was not the circumstance itself, but God's Word in the circumstance. Would they believe God's promise of provision despite what they saw and felt in their situation? God's test to us is the same today: Will we believe His Word despite what we see and feel?

Let's look at other examples of God's testing. The Bible says that God tested Abraham. *"After these events, God tested and proved Abraham"* (Genesis 22:1, AMP). If we keep reading, we learn that God told Abraham to offer up his son Isaac as a sacrifice. God didn't take Isaac from Abraham to see how

Abraham would respond. That's how many people explain God's testing. They believe He takes precious things away from people to see their response. Yet, the scripture clearly states that God's test to Abraham was His Word: "Will you obey Me?" "Will you do what I ask you to do?"

You may wonder, "Why did God need to test Abraham since He already knew how Abraham would respond?" God did not *need* to test Abraham. Based on what scripture says about the character of God—He is good and good means good—we can assume that Abraham was benefited by this opportunity to demonstrate his faith through obeying God's Word. Abraham was so certain that Isaac was the son God had promised him that *"Abraham assumed that if Isaac died, God was able to bring him back to life again"* (Hebrews 11:19, NLT).

Also, many events and people in the Old Testament are pictures that foreshadow Jesus and His work on the Cross. Abraham's sacrifice of his only son was such an event. Abraham loved his son but was willing to sacrifice him, just as God the Father loved His Son, Jesus, and was willing to sacrifice Him to redeem mankind. *"He* (Abraham) *considered that God is able to raise men even from the dead; from which he* (Abraham) *also received him* (Isaac) *back as a type"* (Hebrews 11:19, NASB). Isaac was a type of Christ and the offering of Isaac in sacrifice was a picture of the offering of Jesus on Calvary. When Abraham told Isaac they were going to make a sacrifice, the son asked his father where they would get a lamb to slay. Abraham replied, *"My son, God will provide himself a lamb for a burnt offering"* (Genesis 22:8). Although God did provide Abraham and Isaac with a ram to sacrifice that day, Abraham was speaking of the coming of the Only Son of God, Jesus, whom God the Father would give to be the sacrificial Lamb for the sins of men.

Scripture says that God tested Joseph with His Word. *"He sent a man before them, even Joseph, who was sold as a servant. His feet they hurt with fetters; he was laid in chains of iron and his soul entered into the iron, Until his word [to his cruel brothers] came true, until the word of the Lord tried and tested him"* (Psalm 105:17-19, AMP). God promised Joseph greatness, but that promise seemed thwarted when Joseph's brothers sold him into slavery and he ended up in prison falsely accused of rape (Genesis 37–50). God's test was not the afflictive circumstances Joseph endured. The test was: Would Joseph continue to believe God's promise of greatness despite how impossible his circumstances looked while he was enslaved and put in prison? In the same way, God's test to you and me is not our circumstances. God's test is His Word in the midst of our circumstances. Will we continue to believe and obey what God says despite how things look, despite what we see, and despite how we feel?

DO TRIALS MAKE US PATIENT?

Many Christians believe that God sends us trials to give us patience. I've heard well meaning Christians say: "Whatever you do, don't pray for patience. If you do, God will see to it that difficult circumstances and people come your way to make you more patient." Think about it. We all have tests and trials. If they make us patient, then why aren't we all patient?

According to the Bible, trials don't *create* patience, trials give us an opportunity to *exercise* patience. Patience is a fruit of the Spirit that is resident within the recreated spirit of every Christian (Galatians 5:22-23). It's a spiritual strength that enables us to endure and remain steadfast in the midst of life's challenges. Difficulties, tests, and trials give us an opportunity to exercise or draw out the patience that is within us, helping us to stand our ground and hold steady until we see victory in our situation. James 1:2-3 says, *"Consider it wholly joyful, my brethren, whenever you are enveloped in or encounter trials of any sort or fall into various temptations. Be assured and understand that the trial and proving of your faith* **bring out** *endurance and steadfastness and patience"* (AMP).

Let's compare patience to physical exercise. Exercise does not create muscles, but instead gives you an opportunity to work and strengthen the muscles you already have. In the same way, trials do not create patience. They give you an opportunity to exercise and strengthen the patience you possess because you are born again.

GOD TRIES THE RIGHTEOUS

Perhaps you're thinking, "What about Psalm 11:5, which says God tests the righteous?" That verse is a line from a prayer David prayed when King Saul was trying to destroy him. Not only was David's life in jeopardy, he was being falsely accused of plotting to take Saul's throne.

David began his prayer by declaring, despite how bad things look, *"In the Lord put I my trust...the Lord is in his holy temple, the Lord's throne is in heaven"* (Psalm 11:1,4). David then proclaimed: God is aware of everything that is happening. *"His eyes behold, his eyelids try, the children of men. The Lord trieth the righteous"* (Psalm 11:4-5). The words "try" and "trieth" are the same word in the original Hebrew, meaning to "test metal." When used figuratively, the word means to "investigate" or "examine." *"He watches everything closely, examining everyone on earth. The Lord examines both the righteous and the wicked"* (Psalm 11:4-5, NLT). The idea is not that God is *testing* men, but rather that He is *watching* men. David was stating that God knew he had not acted unrighteously in regard to King Saul and would therefore help him. David was relying on the fact that God sees everything, including the hearts of both himself and Saul, and eventually, justice would prevail in his situation (Psalm 11:6-7).

David's words are an expression of a common theme in scripture: God sees the hearts of men, knows their innermost thoughts and motives, and deals with them accordingly (1 Samuel 16:7; 1 Chronicles 28:9; Jeremiah 17:10) These verses have nothing to do with God orchestrating circumstances to test His people.

TRIALS ARE NOT GOLDEN

Despite the many non-Biblical ideas Christians have about tests and trials—including entire songs about God giving us trials of gold to test us—trials are not golden. Trials are the result of sin in the earth and the work of Satan. They come to steal the Word of God from us and destroy our faith. It is our faith that is more precious than gold.

God does not send trials to test us, strengthen us, or make us more patient. God tests us and strengthens us with His Word. He gives us patience through the new birth, and then, in the midst of troubles, He strengthens us inwardly by His Spirit through His Word to help us exercise that ability to endure as we respond to the difficulties of life.

AN EXAMPLE OF TRIBULATION

*L*et's look at an incident in the New Testament and see how the things we have discussed apply to a difficult circumstance. Jesus and His disciples climbed into a boat to cross the Sea of Galilee where they encountered a terrible storm and the boat began to take on water. Jesus was asleep in the back of the vessel. The disciples awoke Him and He stilled the storm. Had Jesus not intervened, they probably would have died (Mark 4:35-41).

WHY?

This incident brings up the question all of us struggle with in hard times: "Why did this storm happen?" We know that God didn't send the storm. How do we know? Jesus said that God is better than the best earthly father. A good earthly parent wouldn't send a storm and put His children in a life-threatening situation on purpose. Also, Jesus stopped the storm. If God sent the storm, then Jesus undid the work of God by stopping it. That's a house divided against itself and God is not working against Himself.

Did God allow the storm? God allowed the storm in the same way that He allows people to sin and go to hell. He was not for it or behind it in any way. Destructive storms are part of life in a world damaged by sin. They are one of the consequences of the choice Adam and Eve made in the Garden of Eden. Before sin occurred, the earth was watered by a mist (Genesis 2:6). Killer storms did not exist. Adam's sin unleashed a curse in the earth—a curse that includes destructive storms.

Did Satan send the storm? We can't tell from the scriptures. But as the first rebel in the universe, he was indirectly responsible for it and, as we'll see, he was at work in the storm. God didn't permit the devil to work against the disciples for a sovereign purpose. God and Satan are not working together. The devil isn't God's hit man. The devil isn't God's special chastening agent reserved for His choicest servants. And God doesn't "have the devil on a leash." A deadly storm arose on the Sea of Galilee because that's life in a sin cursed earth.

In this incident, we see a clear example of how Satan works in and through life's challenges to steal the Word of God from men. By the time the disciples were caught in this deadly storm, Jesus had already told them that God is a Father who is better than the best earthly father. He had told them that their Heavenly Father cares for the birds and the flowers and that they matter more than birds or flowers. Jesus let them know that if they needed bread, the Father wouldn't give them a stone. If they needed fish, He wouldn't give them a snake. And by performing many healings and deliverances, Jesus had already clearly demonstrated the power of the Father to help His children.

In the midst of this life-threatening situation, we see that all the wonderful words from the lips of Jesus were stolen from the disciples. Their first statement to Jesus was, "Jesus, don't you care about us? We're about to die!" They made no mention of the love and care of their heavenly Father for them. They made no mention of the power of their Father demonstrated through Jesus. Why? Because the Word of God had been stolen from them.

How was the Word stolen? The disciples were faced with a circumstance that made it look as though God didn't care about them. When looking at a dangerous storm that was getting worse, the disciples let the Word of God about a good heavenly Father slip away from them. They agreed with what the circumstance said instead of what God said.

BEWARE OF LIES

It's not clear from scripture if the storm was instigated directly by the devil or if it was simply a result of the curse in the earth because of Adam's sin. In one sense, the direct cause of the storm really doesn't matter. The devil was still active in the situation. The disciples' own words when they cried out to Jesus show us that they had accepted lies from the devil about their situation. The devil doesn't work on us through raw power, he works on us through lies. His only power over us is to get us to believe and act on lies. That is how the devil steals the Word of God from us. He lies to us. He contradicts God's Word to us. In the midst of tribulation, persecution, and affliction, the devil whispers to our minds: "God doesn't care about you. He's forgotten about you. You're going down."

Nowhere does the Bible tell us to beware of the power of the devil. Instead we're told to beware of his mental strategies. *"Put on God's whole armor...that you may be able successfully to stand up against [all] the strategies and the deceits of the devil"* (Ephesians 6:11, AMP). God's armor is His Word. *"His*

99

faithful promises are your armor" (Psalm 91:4, TLB). We must take God's armor, His Word, and expose and resist the lies of the devil in the midst of our circumstances.

Some of the devil's most powerful lies have to do with God's character—what God is really like. Since the beginning of human history, one of the devil's most effective strategies has been to attack God's character. This is the tactic he used on Eve in the Garden of Eden. God told Adam and Eve not to eat from the tree of the knowledge of good and evil, warning that they would die if they did so. When the devil approached Eve he contradicted God. *"You will not surely die' the serpent said to the woman"* (Genesis 3:4, NIV). Then, Satan directly challenged God's character: *"For God knows that when you eat of it your eyes will be opened, and you will be like God, knowing good and evil"* (Genesis 3:5, NIV). In other words, the devil told Eve, "God has been holding out on you. The reason God doesn't want you to eat that fruit is because He is a withholder and a depriver. He knows it would be good for you to eat from this tree. God is actually your problem." The devil uses the same tactics on us today.

OUR FATHER WILL HELP US

Let's go back to the disciples in the boat on the Sea of Galilee. After Jesus stopped the storm, He rebuked His disciples: *"And he said unto them, Why are ye so fearful? How is it that ye have no faith?"* (Mark 4:40). Notice, Jesus calls their reaction to the storm "no faith." What did they do? How did they react to the storm? I have heard preachers say that Jesus was upset with His disciples in this incident because He expected them to stop the storm. I don't doubt there is truth to that. But I believe Jesus was upset with them for an even more basic reason. In light of all He had taught them and showed them up to this point about their Heavenly Father, they still doubted God's care for them in the midst of the storm. Jesus expected them to respond with faith in their Father: "This situation looks really bad. We don't know what to do. But we know we have a good Father in heaven who loves us and cares for us and He will get us through this storm."

Note the connection between accurate knowledge of God's character and effective faith. You can't have strong faith in someone you don't fully trust. That is why the devil works so hard to persuade men to believe that God does bad to people. Notice also that because the disciples were not grounded in the knowledge of God's character, they sided in with what their sight and feelings told them when circumstances made it look as though God didn't care about them. Jesus had mercy on the disciples and helped them anyway. But based on their reaction to the storm, we can see why it's vital to develop an accurate picture of God's character from the Bible.

CONCLUSION

Why is the information in this book important? As I said at the beginning, you must understand that your troubles do not come from God. If we believe that God is behind our troubles, we'll fall prey to one of two destructive results: passivity or bitterness. Passivity sets in when we mistakenly think our trials come from God and, as a result, we accept challenges in our lives that we should resist in the name of Jesus. Bitterness and anger toward God can also spring up when we think God has orchestrated or is in favor of the difficulties we face.

At this point in time, no one can fully explain why evil is present in the world or why pain and suffering are such a part of human existence. However, as you face the hardships of life, you need to know beyond a shadow of a doubt that your troubles do not come from God. That knowledge will relieve you of the anguish that comes from wondering, "Why is God allowing this trial?" or "What is God trying to accomplish by sending suffering my way?" These questions undermine your confidence in God, who is your source of help in times of trouble. Accurate knowledge of God's character can help you face the hardships of life and shut down the "why" questions.

If you know that God is good and good means good, and if you're fully convinced that God is not behind your troubles in any way, then you can face the difficulties of life and say with confidence: "What I'm facing right now is really bad, but I know these awful circumstances didn't come from God. My Father is good and He would never be behind something like this. Why is this happening to me? Because that's life in a sin cursed earth. But God will get me through until He gets me out.

God will cause this to serve His purposes, which are maximum glory to Himself and maximum good to as many people as possible, and He will bring genuine good out of genuine bad. God is good…and good means good."

OTES

THE WORKS OF JESUS

1. These are some of the verses that state Jesus spoke the words of His Father and did the works of His Father by the power of the Father in Him: John 4:34; 5:36; 7:16; 8:28-29; 9:4; 10:32; 14:10; 17:4

SATAN

2. Satan is an angel. God created angels to obey, serve, and worship Him (Job 38:7; Psalm 103:20-21). The angels were given wisdom, strength, and beauty (2 Samuel 14:20; Ezekiel 28:12; Psalm 103:20). Scripture suggests they had different roles, privileges, and responsibilities. Before God created the material world and man, He ruled over an invisible, spiritual kingdom populated with angelic beings.

Ezekiel 28:12-19 speaks of an angel (a cherub) called Lucifer who had great beauty and ministered in the presence of God before His throne. But Lucifer became proud. Isaiah 14:12-14 describes the events that led to the fall of this beautiful angelic being. The prophet begins by talking about an earthly king, the King of Babylon (Isaiah 14:4-11), and then transitions to an unseen power (Lucifer) working through the king. Lucifer's name means "brightness" in Hebrew. He tried to assert his will over God and become king over God. Lucifer became God's adversary. Satan means "adversary." He offered himself as an alternate king and enticed numerous angels to join him in rebellion, setting up his own counterfeit kingdom in the unseen realm. All the angels who followed Lucifer in rebellion are subjects of Satan's kingdom.

When God created the earth and man, He gave men dominion on the earth (Genesis 1:26-28). God instructed the first man, Adam, to refrain from eating the fruit of the tree of the knowledge of good and evil to provide man with an opportunity to express his recognition of and submission to the authority of God, the rightful King of the Universe. Satan, through the serpent, enticed Adam and Eve to eat from the forbidden tree (Genesis 2:16-17; Genesis 3:1-6). Through their disobedience to the King, Adam and Eve submitted themselves to the rule of Satan. Satan's kingdom, which up to that time had only existed in the heavenlies, was now established on earth (Luke 4:6; 2 Corinthians 4:4). His kingdom is characterized by lawlessness, unrighteousness, darkness, and deceit. Satan hates what God loves.

Satan, as a created being, is not omnipresent. He carries out the work of his kingdom through the other fallen angels (known as devils or demons). His kingdom has organization and rank (Ephesians 2:2; 6:12). Principalities are beings that, through people, rule nations and large areas of the world. Powers are of slightly lesser rank, probably ministers associated with government. Rulers of the darkness of this world suggests beings with a ministry of deception, focusing especially on people who influence the thought life of others. Wicked spirits in the heavenlies are innumerable beings (demons) who interact with people, stirring up grosser sins and deceptions, animal passions, sensual desires, and religious deceptions. The devil and his invisible followers influence humanity through deception, through oppression, obsession, and possession—all of which produce much of the hell and heartache that occurs in the world.

God has judged the devil, but he is not yet subjugated. The devil's authority over the human race was broken at the Cross of Christ, but he has not yet been removed from human contact. At the return of Jesus Christ to this earth, every knee will bow and every tongue confess that Jesus is Lord—including the devil—and he will be permanently removed from interacting with people (John 12:31; Isaiah 14:15-17; Revelation 20:10). Right now the devil still has some time left on this earth and he goes about seeking people to devour (1 Peter 5:8).

In this book, the term "devil" is used as an inclusive word meaning Satan himself and the multitudes of demons who inhabit the invisible realm on this earth. The devil does not cause every hardship in life, but he and his demons are actively at work influencing the hearts and minds of men to keep them blinded to the reality of God and His kingdom and to motivate them to continue to act in ways that are contrary to God. In addition, the hardships and sufferings of life are here because of sin (beginning with Adam's sin) and are ultimately traceable back to Satan as the first rebel in the universe.

ROMANS 9

3. The subject under discussion in Romans 9, 10, and 11 is God's dealings with the nation of Israel. These chapters show God's sovereignty and justice in His dealings with Israel. They aren't an explanation of suffering in the lives of individual people. Consider this brief summary of Romans 9, which contains several verses that are frequently misunderstood and misapplied in regard to God's sovereignty.

In Romans 9:1-5, Paul pours out his heart over his people, the Jews. He has great sorrow because most of them have rejected Christ. Paul states that even though Israel as a whole has not responded to the gospel, the Word of God has not failed. The Gentiles have become children of Abraham through faith in Christ (Romans 9:6-8). Then Paul explains why it isn't unfair of God to make people who aren't physical descendants of Abraham His own. Paul states that God has purposefully picked out a specific line through which the Redeemer would eventually come, beginning with the call of Abraham (Romans 9:9-12). God promised Abraham and Sarah a son. Sarah was barren, so in response to His promise, she and Abraham devised their own plan to bring that promise to pass. Abraham lay with Hagar, Sarah's maid servant, and they produced Ishmael. Their attempt to bring God's promise to pass their own way didn't stop God's plan. God had chosen Isaac, not Ishmael, as the seed to whom and through whom the promise of the Redeemer would pass (Genesis 26:1-5). Many years later, Isaac married Rebecca who became pregnant with twins, Esau and Jacob. Before the twins were born, God chose Jacob as the seed through whom the promises made to Abraham would come to pass.

In Romans 9:13, Paul quotes Malachi 1:2-3 where God says, *"Yet I loved Jacob, And I hated Esau."* If you don't understand the context, this verse appears to contradict other scriptures that say God loves all men. Paul is speaking about nations in Romans 9:11-13, not individuals: *"(For the children being not yet born, neither having done any good or evil, that the purpose of God according to election might stand, not of works, but of him that calleth;) It was said unto her, the elder shall serve the younger. As it is written, Jacob have I loved, but Esau have I hated."* Jacob is the nation of Israel and Esau is the nation of Edom. The word "children" isn't in the original text; "nation" actually makes more sense in this context. The nation of Israel descended from Jacob and the nation of Edom descended from Esau. When Rebecca was pregnant with Jacob and Esau, God spoke to her and told her she had two nations in her womb (Genesis 25:22-23). The point is, neither group did anything to deserve being made God's special people. It was up to God to choose the one through whom the Redeemer would ultimately come and He chose Jacob (the nation of Israel).

God "hated" Edom (Esau) because, as we study their history, we find that the nation of Edom continually opposed the nation of Israel (Jacob). "Hated" means "loved less." The Amplified Translation makes this meaning more clear: *"As it is written, Jacob have I loved, but Esau have I hated [held in relative disregard in comparison with My feeling for Jacob]"* (Romans 9:13).

In Romans 9:14-16, Paul asks and answers the question: "Is God unrighteous because He put His blessings on one particular group of people—namely, the descendants of Abraham, Isaac, and Jacob?" Paul goes on to answer "No, God can bless whomever He chooses." Romans 9:15 is a quote from Exodus 33:19 where God states that He'll have mercy on whomever He desires, including the Jews who deserved to be cut off for their wicked idolatry in Exodus 32. In other words, it was up to God as to who would be the line through which the blessings of Abraham would pass. God, the sovereign Lord, has the right to bless whomever He chooses.

As we continue in Romans, we come to another verse that has also been widely misunderstood and misused. Romans 9:17 says, *"For the scripture saith unto Pharaoh, Even for this same purpose have I raised thee up, that I might show my power in thee, and that my name might be declared throughout all the earth."* Some say this verse means that God raised Pharaoh up just so He could crush him—and God may do the same thing to us because He is the Potter and we are the clay. But that is not correct. Verse 17 is a reference to Exodus 9:13-16 where God let Pharaoh know it was His sovereign kindness that had kept Pharaoh and the Egyptians from being destroyed by past plagues. A little further in Exodus, the scripture says, *"For by now I could have put forth My hand and have struck you and your people with pestilence, and you would have been cut off from the earth. But for this very purpose have I let you live, that I might show you My power, and that My name may be declared throughout all the earth"* (Exodus 9:15-16, AMP). The original Hebrew language says, "I have caused thee to stand." God, in His kindness, had preserved the Egyptians so that He could have a further chance to show them that He, Jehovah, was and is the only true God. As we referenced in Chapter 5, some Egyptians responded to God and were saved as a result of the mighty demonstrations of power He used in Egypt to deliver Israel from slavery (Exodus 8:19; 9:20; 12:37-38; Joshua 2:9-11).

Paul then concludes that God, according to His own will and wisdom, gives His blessings to one part of mankind (Jews in the Old Testament and Gentiles in the New Testament) while He allows another part to experience the consequences of their sins (the Egyptians in the Old Testament and the Jews in the New Testament). Romans 9:18 says, *"Therefore hath he mercy on whom he will have mercy, and whom he will he hardened."* Some people mistakenly take this verse to mean that God sometimes hardens people's hearts because He is the Potter and can do whatever He wants. After all, they say, God hardened Pharaoh's heart. However, the phrase "Whom He will He hardeneth" is a Hebraism, which we reviewed in Chapter 5. In the Hebrew language, God is said to do what He only allows. If we read carefully all the comments about Pharaoh, it's clear that Pharaoh hardened his own heart toward God (1 Samuel 6:6) just as the children of Israel hardened their own hearts toward God in rejecting Jesus (Matthew 13:13-15; John 12:37-38).

In Romans 9:19-20, Paul begins to deal with several questions: *"You will say to me, Why then does He still find fault and blame us [for sinning]? For who can resist and withstand His will? But who are you, a mere man, to criticize and contradict and answer back to God? Will what is formed say to him that formed it, Why have you made me thus?"* (AMP). Paul says no one has the right to ask this. In context, "what is formed" is nations. Paul then quotes from the parable of the Potter in Jeremiah 18:1-10, which refers to God's dealings with Israel. The point of the parable is that as the Sovereign Potter, God has the right to accept or reject Israel based on their faithfulness to Him. The parable has nothing to do with God molding individuals through tragedies and trials.

If you don't take these passages in context, it's possible to draw incorrect conclusions. Some people maintain that Romans 9 says God makes some people vessels of wrath meant for destruction and some people vessels of mercy meant for glory because He is the Potter and we are the clay. Paul goes on to say in Romans 9:22, *"What if God, willing to show his wrath, and to make his power known, endured with much longsuffering the vessels of wrath fitted to destruction."* Vessels of wrath are Pharaoh (and the Egyptians) and Israel. Both groups were guilty of sin before God—Egypt through idol worship and Israel through their rejection of their Messiah. Both had hardened their hearts in the face of mighty demonstrations of God's grace, power, and patience, fitting themselves for destruction. In Romans 9:23-24, Paul goes on to say: *"And he has a right to take others such as ourselves, who have been made for pouring the riches of his glory into, whether we are Jews or Gentiles, and to be kind to us so that everyone can see how very great his glory is"* (TLB).

111

Paul concludes his argument by stating that God as the Potter has the right to offer salvation to the Gentiles through faith now that the Jews have rejected His offer of salvation.

These verses can't mean that God makes some people for destruction and others for glory because the New Testament teaches that the kind of vessels we are as individuals is up to us and is determined by our responses to God and His Word. 2 Timothy 2:20-21 says: *"But in a great house there are not only vessels of gold and of silver, but also of wood and of earth; and some to honour, and some to dishonour. If a man therefore purge himself from these, he shall be a vessel unto honour, sanctified, and meet for the master's use, and prepared unto every good work."*

1 Thessalonians 4:3-4 says: *"For this is the will of God, even your sanctification, that ye should abstain from fornication: That every one of you should know how to possess his vessel in sanctification and honour."* Whether you are a vessel of wrath or a vessel of honor is not God's decision. It's up to you.

CAUSATIVE VERBS USED IN A PERMISSIVE SENSE

4. This information can be verified in *Figures of Speech Used in the Bible* by E.W. Bullinger. Bullinger says that when a causative verb is used in a permissive sense, it is idiomatic (or used as an idiom) and that context determines if a verb is causative or permissive (Page 823). An idiom is an expression whose meaning is not predictable from the usual grammatical rules of language or from the usual meanings of the words used in the phrase (*Webster's Universal College Dictionary*). We have idioms in the English language. The phrase, "It's raining cats and dogs," is an idiom meaning, "It's raining heavily."

112

Normally, the words "cats" and "dogs" have nothing to do with rainfall. But when they are used this way, everyone who speaks English understands from the context what is being said. It is the same in the Hebrew language.

Clarke's Commentary, Matthew–Revelation, by Adam Clarke, also verifies that in the Hebrew language causative verbs were used in a permissive sense. Clarke, in discussing the Lord's Prayer, refers to the line "And lead us not into temptation" as a "mere Hebraism; God is said to do a thing which he only permits or suffers to be done" (Page 87).

An early edition of *Young's Analytical Concordance of the Bible* has a section in the Appendix that discusses this verb usage. The book is out of print. The same author, Robert Young, wrote *Hints to Bible Interpretation*, which also deals with these verbs. It also is out of print.

SUFFERING PERSECUTION

5. Other examples in the Book of Acts of suffering persecution for preaching the gospel include: Acts 4:3-21; 6:9-15; 7:54-60; 8:1-4; 9:1-2; 12:1-11.

Made in the USA
Monee, IL
07 March 2020